Actions

International Library of Philosophy

Editor: Ted Honderich

A Catalogue of books already published in the *International Library of Philosophy* will be found at the end of this volume

Actions

Jennifer Hornsby
Fellow of Corpus Christi College, Oxford

ROUTLEDGE & KEGAN PAUL
London, Boston and Henley

First published in 1980
by Routledge & Kegan Paul Ltd
39 Storet, London WC1E 7DD,
Broadway House, Newtown Road,
Henley-on-Thames, Oxon RG9 1EN and
9 Park Street, Boston Mass. 02108, USA
Set in IBM Press Roman 10 on 12 pt. by
Hope Services, Abingdon
and printed in Great Britain by
Lowe & Brydone Ltd
Thetford, Norfolk

British Library Cataloguing in Publication Data

Hornsby, Jennifer

Actions – (International library of philosophy).
1. Act (Philosophy)
I. Title II. Series
128'.3 B104.A35 79-42756

ISBN 0 7100 0451 6
ISBN 0 7100 0452 4 Pbk

CONTENTS

	Preface	vi
One:	Actions and Bodily Movements	1
Appendix:	On Goldman's Account of Individuating Actions	
Two:	Bodily Movements and Muscle Contractions	20
Appendix:	On Thalberg's Account of Individuating Actions	
Three:	Acting and Trying to Act	33
Four:	Aberrations of Volitionalists	46
Five:	Basic Action and Causation	66
Six:	Basic Action and Teleology	78
Seven:	Action and Causation	89
Eight:	Knowledge of Action	102
Nine:	Action and Perception	111
Appendix A:	On Some Causative Transitive Verbs	124
Appendix B:	Logical Form, Event Individuation	133
	Bibliography	138
	Index	144

PREFACE

I completed a first draft of this book during my tenure of the Sarah Smithson Research Fellowship at Newnham College, Cambridge, and I thank the College for support.

I gratefully acknowledge the help of advice and criticism from David Pears, David Wiggins and Bernard Williams.

Anyone who knows Donald Davidson's writings in the philosophy of action will realize that my debt to his conception of the subject is insufficiently recorded even by the numerous references I make to his work.

I

ACTIONS AND BODILY MOVEMENTS

1

There is a thesis about human action that can be summed up in the formula 'All actions are bodily movements'. But this is ambiguous. Read in one way, it expresses an important (if not exceptionless) truth; but on another perfectly natural interpretation, I should maintain, it is definitely false.

The first part of this essay shows how much it matters to distinguish between the two statements that the ambiguous sentence makes. The present chapter will be devoted to the character of the difference between them, and to defending the true statement by contrast with the false one. The result is a view about actions that is surprising on the face of it. But I hope to make it seem less surprising by giving two more arguments for it (Chapters Two and Three), and then to show, through discussion of some general questions about action, how unsurprising are its consequences (Chapters Four to Eight).

We shall see that ambiguity is not the only affliction of the claim that actions are bodily movements. Though it is a claim about particular actions, it is apt to be confused with a claim about kinds of actions. The confusion arises from a pervasive misunderstanding of the phrases we employ when we begin to talk about action in a general way, and speak of 'doing something' or 'performing an action'.

The aim of the book as a whole is to investigate the nature of actions seen as revelations of the human mind. But I think that we have to start the investigation with some points that make it clear what is meant when it is said that all (physical) actions are movements of the body.

2

2.1 'Move' belongs to a class of English verbs that occur both transitively (i.e. with grammatical objects) and intransitively (without objects), the two sorts of occurrence being related in sense in a certain systematic way. If Jane melted_T the chocolate, then the chocolate melted_I. If Mr Brown grows_T lettuces in his garden, then lettuces grow_I in Mr Brown's garden. If John moved_T his body, then his body moved_I. Subscripts 'T' and 'I' are used to distinguish transitive from intransitive here and throughout; and a verb V is in the intended class if, and only if, it supports inferences on the following pattern[1]:

FROM: $a\ V_T\ b$ TO: $b\ V_I$

Occurring as verbs in whole sentences, these words create no ambiguities for the most part, because the presence of a (surface structure) object word is generally a reliable and adequate sign of a transitive use (in deep structure). But in nominal phrases there tend to be two readings.[2] Does 'the melting of the chocolate' describe someone's melting_T the chocolate, or does it describe the chocolate's melting_I? When it is claimed that all actions are movements of the body, is it being said that every action consists in a moving_T by a mover of his body? Or is the claim that all actions are bodies' movements_I?

If the latter claim is intended, it is *prima facie* implausible. Actions

[1] All the verbs that consistently support inferences of this sort fail to support any converse inference from intransitive to transitive, and this distinguishes them from other kinds of verbs that have transitive and intransitive occurrences. See Appendix A for further details.

The ambiguity in 'move' has been noted by philosophers before (most explicitly and most recently by Thalberg, 1977, p. 55).

[2] There are exceptions to both these generalizations.

(a) Whole sentences may be ambiguous, owing to a phenomenon that linguists call Object Deletion, by which a transitive verb loses its object in surface structure. Thus a verb may sometimes be interpretable as the superficial remnant of a transitive or as a genuine intransitive. **Examples.** 'A cannibal is cooking': is it that he's cooking_T something, or is he the victim – now cooking_I? 'The first man to move goes inside': the first man to move_T his body, or the first man('s body) to move_I? (Of course it will very likely be the same man either way in this case.)

(b) Nominal phrases may be unambiguous, because some 'derived' nominals have only an intransitive sense. (It seems that if a verb takes a nominalizing suffix of Latin origin, viz. '-tion', '-al' or '-ment' (e.g. 'alter', 'move') then the nominal is ambiguous; but otherwise (e.g. 'change', 'turn') it cannot be understood transitively at all. Cp. Smith, 1972.)

occur when we do things (even if we have to do fairly remarkable things for our doings to be dignified, outside of philosophy, with the description *actions*). And the sort of answer we expect to the question 'What did he do?' is not 'His body moved' ('His arm rose', 'His knee bent'), but rather 'He moved his body', ('He raised his arm', 'He bent his knee'). It is the same when we go beyond the agent's body to describe his action: what he did, we say, was melt_T the chocolate; and we cannot say that what he did was the chocolate melted_I. So it appears that if there is to be any hope of truth in an identification of actions with bodily movements, then they must be movements_T, not movements_I, that are actions – his movings_T of his body, not his body's movings_I.

This is how I come to accept at most one reading of the claim that every action is a bodily movement. I deny that any action is a bodily movement_I.

2.2 We should know better what is going on in the argument above if we could gain a better understanding of the question 'What did he do?'.

The phrase 'do something' can mislead, because it can sound as if it reported both an event that is a *doing* and a separate event that is a *something* done. But that cannot be how it behaves. If I raise my arm at some time, raise my arm is something I do then, and my doing something then is my raising my arm then. But *what* I do – raise my arm – is not a particular event that happens at a time: the only event mentioned here is my raising of my arm.

The example suggests that we should think of 'do something' as a sort of schematic verb. *Do something* is generic; *raise my arm*, or *eat a cream bun*, or *pay the bill* is the specification. In any particular case of someone's doing something, and for any thing done, his action (if any) is his doing that thing, and in knowing what that thing is, we know what kind of action there is. Raise his arm is one thing a person may do; and if we know that that is what he does, then we know that his action was of a certain kind, that his action was his raising his arm. (**Question**: How is it that expressions like 'raise his arm' can supplant the *whole* of the phrase 'do something', but can also give instances of what is done [as in 'What he did was raise his arm'] and replace *only* the word 'something'? **Answer**: Here as elsewhere 'do' is auxiliary.)

This account presupposes a general view of the function of verbs – as words that are used to report the occurrence of events, events being the things of which nominal phrases like 'his raising of his arm' are true. But the best means to put the view to the test is to see whether good sense can be made of speaking consistently and explicitly as if it were correct, and the whole of this essay is one such test. Throughout it, I shall use terms that denote events if they denote anything as if they denoted dated, unrepeatable particulars; and I hope that the intelligibility of what I say may be taken as evidence – indirect but copious – for the existence of such things.[3] (Compare Davidson on events (1969b) and (1971b), and on logical form (1967a). But the details of the form of action sentences can be left open here: see Appendix B.)

I do not say that 'event' and 'action' are words that are used exclusively of particulars ('act', at least, is most often used of universals); but for clarity's sake I shall use them only in that way myself. In this usage, actions are people's doings of things, and what is done is never an action. Philosophers who talk about 'doing *x*' or 'doing an *A*' may confuse particular actions with the things done in acting. But English makes it clear enough that there is a categorial difference between them; and by reserving 'action' for the doings, we simply insist that that difference remain as sharp as we find it.[4]

The remarks about 'do something' help us understand what it is to answer the question 'What did he do?'. The person who asks that

[3] It must be acknowledged that many phrases with a form superficially similar to that of 'his raising of his arm' do not denote events. I am inclined to think that some nominals (e.g. 'my eating of a cream bun') unambiguously denote events, and that, where such event-denoting nominals can be found, there are nominals of slightly different form (in this case 'my eating a cream bun') which need not denote events. (Whether tokens of this other nominal denote events or not will usually be determinable in context.) But whatever the subtleties of the truth about nominals may be, there is enough (implicit) agreement about which token expressions denote events if any do for it to be possible to test the view about verbs and events.

[4] There may be uses of 'what he did' which refer to particulars; or at least it may be that philosophers have so often used 'what he did' meaning it to refer to his doing what he did that we now sometimes understand 'what he did' as referring to a particular. If that is so, there is ambiguity in 'what he did', and then my claim will be that it is worth taking pains to disambiguate.

I speak, as other English speakers do, as if we were committed to the existence of the things we do. Whether we accept that that gives us reason to think that there really are such universals as things done is on a par with the question whether we accept that there are things had because we find sentences like 'Wisdom is something he has'. I do not attempt to answer these ontological questions (cp. Chapter Five § 2.3).

question is seeking to discover a kind under which an action of *a* can be subsumed, and is to be answered with a sentence that subsumes an action of *a* under a kind. But the usual way to say what kind of action there was is to say that there was an action of a certain kind. So if we can answer with 'He moved his finger', but never with 'His finger moved', then that does indeed suggest that some actions are bodily movements$_T$, and that no actions are bodily movements$_I$.

2.3 Actions can sometimes be identified with bodily movements$_T$. Actions can never be identified with bodily movements$_I$. I shall be careful to treat these as two separate claims.

Someone might think that it was obvious that bodily movements$_T$ are not the same as bodily movements$_I$, on the grounds that the truth-conditions of 'He moved$_T$ his body' and 'His body moved$_I$' are different, so that *what it is to be a bodily movement*$_T$ must be different from *what it is to be a bodily movement*$_I$. But this does not show that we can proceed from the identity of an action with a bodily movement$_T$ to the non-identity of that action with a bodily movement$_I$. This tells us about the difference of the concepts of *movement*$_T$ and *movement*$_I$, and it is simply a mistake to think that we can go directly from a difference between two senses or two concepts to a difference in any of the particulars that fall under those concepts.

In the case of continuants such a mistake will usually be transparent. Who will say that no giraffe is the same as any animal because *what it is to be a giraffe* is different from *what it is to be an animal?* It is when events are in question that the invalidity of the transition will sometimes be missed. But actions themselves provide some clear cases. The two action descriptions 'pulling a face' and 'making Lucie laugh' are different in sense, and *what it is to be an action of pulling a face* is different from *what it is to be an action of making Lucie laugh*; but that does not show that every particular pulling of a face is different from any particular making of Lucie laugh, because these descriptions sometimes apply to the very same action.

This is controversial. It depends upon a view about the individuation of actions that I believe we must adopt so soon as we start to make sense of our ordinary talk about action; but others have doubted that. I shall argue in Appendices to this chapter and the next against some rival views of individuation (those of Goldman and Thalberg), claiming that they make nonsense of what we ordinarily say. And I shall complete these preliminaries now with some positive support for the view on which everything in this essay is based.

2.4 If we try to think of identity statements about actions, then examples like these may spring to mind:

> I did the same thing as you.
> He did the same thing today as he did yesterday.

But the remarks about 'do something' will have suggested that such sentences as these cannot be the central concern. Here what are said to be the same are things done: but things done are not particular actions. These sentences indeed help to underline the point about the 'something' in 'do something'. For if there are particular actions (as all of the parties to a dispute about their individuation assume there are), then it is surely a sufficient condition of their difference that one is mine, another yours, or that one happened yesterday, another today. And if what I do and what he does are not particulars, because what I do can be the same as what you do, and what he does is the same today as yesterday, then these sentences say that there was a kind of action of which one of my actions and one of your actions are both instances, and a kind of action which subsumes an action of his of today and an action of his of yesterday. The question about individuation is not a question about kinds, about what it is for things done to be the same, but a question about when it is that someone's doing one thing (his action seen as one kind of doing) is the same as his doing another thing (is the same as his action seen as another kind of doing). In saying that some particular pullings of faces are the same as some actions of making Lucie laugh, I say that sometimes someone's pulling a face is the same as his making Lucie laugh. More specifically, I should claim that there is such an identity when, but only when, he makes Lucie laugh *by* pulling a face. It is this word 'by' that is the cardinal thing.

We can see its role in the controversy from a familiar case due to Anscombe (1957). A man who operates a pump replenishes the water supply of a certain house; he does so by moving his arm, and by doing so he introduces poison into the water supply and poisons the inhabitants. Anscombe herself contends that in any episode of pumping we find an action variously describable as a pumping, a moving of the arm, a replenishing of the water supply, a poisoning of the inhabitants; and so would D'Arcy (1963) and Davidson (1971a). But others maintain that there are no true identities to be asserted using pairs of descriptions from the series 'his moving his arm', 'his operating the pump', . . . ; and they sometimes argue for differentiating the actions on the grounds that 'He replenished the water supply by operating the pump' is true, but that 'He replenished the water supply by poisoning the inhabitants' is false. On those grounds, it is said that we can find a property that an action of poisoning the inhabitants possesses, but that any action of operating the pump lacks – namely the property of standing in a relation expressed by 'by' to some particular replenishing of the water supply. More generally, it is said that 'by' expresses a relation that is asymmetric and irreflexive, which can never hold between identicals, so that any sentence of the form 'He ϕ-d by ψ-ing' must report distinct actions. (The argument is Goldman's 1970, pp. 5–6; 1971, pp. 762–3; and Goldman believes in making more distinctions between actions than some of the other opponents of Anscombe. But even those opponents who are prepared to assert many identities that Goldman would deny take it to be a sufficient condition of the distinctness of his ϕ-ing and his ψ-ing that he ϕ-d by ψ-ing.)

If it were sound, this argument would settle the matter against Anscombe and Davidson and me. And except by denying Leibniz's Law, no one who thinks that on some occasion the pumper's poisoning the inhabitants was the same as his operating of the pump can hold *both* 'His replenishing of the water supply was by his operating of the pump' *and* 'His replenishing of the water supply was not by his poisoning of the inhabitants'. But in this explicit statement, the problem comes to the surface. Why should anyone want to say either of these things? It is not clear that they make sense. Seeing that, we should wonder what reason there might be for the assumption which sets the argument in motion, that 'by' expresses a relation between events.

It looks as though the function of 'by' is to form verbs out of verbs and verb phrases. We have, for example, the verb 'to replenish the water supply', and from this we can form the more complex verb 'to replenish the water supply by operating a pump': the phrase 'by operating a pump' retains a constant grammatical form as the verb 'replenish' is inflected for person and tense. If that is right, then the sentence 'He replenished the water supply by operating the pump' does not contain any mention of an action of operating the pump – let alone any assertion of a relation between such an action and another. The sentence tells us simply that there was an action of replenishing-the-water-supply-by-operating-the-pump.[5]

If this account of 'by' is too superficial to resolve the debate about identities, it will at least provide a means of formulating the issue. We need to ask whether complex verbs containing the word 'by' can be used to introduce the same actions as their simpler constituent verbs; for instance, whether 'his poisoning the inhabitants by operating the pump' ever describes the same action as 'his poisoning the inhabitants', or describes the same action as 'his operating the pump'.

[5] Kit Fine has put it to me that even if 'by' itself is not a relation between particulars, we can define a relation that does hold between particulars (and then argue for non-identities on the basis of the properties of the new relation). Thus:

$(\mathrm{BY}_{\mathrm{Df}})$ $(\forall x)(\forall y)$(A performed x by performing y iff $\mathrm{BY}_{\mathrm{A}}(x,y)$)

If this definition is to enable us to understand 'BY', then we must understand the left-hand side as a sentence of English. But the left-hand side presupposes the acceptability of the very assumption about 'by'-sentences that I reject. Why should one think that in the phrase 'by ψ-ing' the expression 'ψ-ing' plays the role that 'ϕ' plays in 'He ϕ-ed'? After all, we never say 'He ϕ-ed by he ψ-ed'. If 'He performed x' tells us that there was an action of his, and if when someone ϕ-s by ψ-ing there is only one action needed to verify a sentence that says what he does, then the only intelligible paraphrases of 'by'-sentences using 'perform' are these:

He performed a ϕ-ing by ψ-ing.
He performed x and x was a ϕ-ing by ψ-ing.
He performed something by performing something else.

To assume that in the very last occurrence of 'perform something' here, the word 'something' corresponds to a variable ranging over particular actions is just one way of disregarding my own view that the surface form of 'by'-sentences is some sort of guide to their logical form.

'Perform x', like do x', is a favourite of philosophers. But it is harder to say anything definite about how this phrase is meant to function, because 'perform ——' leads a more promiscuous life than the 'do ——' that philosophers use. Many of the things that we say we perform – symphonies and operations and the like – are neither particular actions nor kinds of action. Usually 'perform an act' appears to work very much like 'do something', so that what is performed is not an action, not something denoted by a phrase like 'his raising his arm'; and if it works like that, then $(\mathrm{BY}_{\mathrm{Df}})$ fails to define a relation between particulars. Now it may be that English will tolerate cognate accusatives on the surface and that we can understand such things as 'He raised his arm a raising' and 'He walked a walk'. If so, then 'perform x' may stand as a schematic verb having as instances certain expressions that join with names of persons to form sentences, and then e.g. 'signalled a signalling' instantiates 'perform x' and 'x' ranges over particulars. But this is still not to say, what $(\mathrm{BY}_{\mathrm{Df}})$ presupposes, that 'by performing x' is similarly intelligible for expressions that join with sentences to form sentences, as 'by waving' can join with 'He signalled' to give 'He signalled by waving'.

My answer is that if 'his poisoning the inhabitants' denotes an action that happened on an occasion when he poisoned the inhabitants by operating a pump, then 'his poisoning the inhabitants by operating the pump' provides us with a fuller story of an action of operating the pump that occurred then. After all, it seems that an action that takes any time to occur is occurring at any moment of that time, and that any moment at which *a*'s action is occurring is a moment when *a* is doing something. But then if the action that is the poisoning of the inhabitants were to have gone on after the action of operating the pump, the pumper would have to have been doing something after he operated the pump. Suppose, though, that the pumper operated the pump just once, and that he dropped dead as soon as his arm left the pumping mechanism. That need have made no difference to whether or not he poisoned the inhabitants. But it would have to have made a difference to when he was doing things: we are inactive after we are dead, so that in this case he wasn't doing anything after he operated the pump. His action of poisoning must then have happened when his action of operating the pump did. (This is not to say that his action of poisoning must have been a poisoning then – cp. Bennett (1973) –, nor that 'He has poisoned the inhabitants' must have been true then. I discuss date and tense in (1979).)

But while he was operating the pump, there was nothing that the pumper was doing that could possibly count as his poisoning the inhabitants, unless it was operating the pump. So his operating of the pump was the same as his action of poisoning the inhabitants. By similar reasoning, his moving his arm was also his doing these things. In the circumstances, moving his arm is something he needs to have been doing if he is to have done these other things. But once he has moved his arm, no further action on his part is called for: even if he were to have dropped dead, he would still have done them. Other things are done by him, but no other doing of his occurs. For, as Davidson puts it, 'The rest is up to nature' (1971a, p. 23).

Such identities show that many actions are thought of as causes of other events. If we find a description that we know picks out an action, but makes allusion to something that occurred at a time when the agent might not have been doing anything (the inhabitants' swallowing poisoned water, say), then the proper conclusion is that what is alluded to is an outcome of the action in terms of which the action is described. But the idea that we speak of many actions as causes of other events has independent plausibility. Lawyers believe that questions about whether persons have done certain things can be reduced to questions about whether they have caused certain other sorts of things, and numerous philosophers have spoken of actions as agents' *bringing things about*. And such explicitly causal language is used in everyday reports of actions too. Suppose that we learn now that the pumper actually killed the inhabitants. Then have we not learned that some action of his brought about their death? But if we know that it was by operating the pump that he killed them, can we not say that it was his operating the pump that brought about their death? But that is to say that there was an action that was his killing them and that was his operating the pump – and we have evidence for the view of individuation direct from the use of 'bring about'.

3

3.1 Each of the principal points of the previous four subsections can be brought to bear upon the interpretation of the sentence I started from, in the interpretation that I accept: 'All actions are bodily movements' (Davidson, 1971a, p. 24).

The word 'move' here is to be understood transitively – 'move$_T$' (§ 2.1). The sentence speaks of actions, or doings, and tells us that they are all doings of a certain kind – the *bodily movement* kind (§ 2.2). This is not to be committed to thinking that none of our actions is not also of some different kind, but only that each particular action can be identified with some movement or other of our bodies (§ 2.3). So we have a wholesale claim about particular identities. It is stronger than that which the earlier argument established, because the earlier argument, based as it was on the use of bodily movement words in answering questions about what has been done, could show no more than that bodily movements$_T$ are among actions; and we have now come to say that bodily movements$_T$ are all the actions there are. But that is supported by the account of individuating actions (§ 2.4).

In many episodes of a person's doing something, he moves$_T$ his body. But having moved his body, there is nothing further that he has to do. Having moved his finger on a light switch, for instance (if turning on a light is something he does), he has already played his part in turning on the light. So we can argue that his movement is his action. But if very often when we act there is a movement, and if always the movement is then the action, then very many actions are movements. This is to say that if we focus on any action and ask about something done 'What did he do in doing it? or 'By doing what did he do it?', then very often it would be possible to answer by describing the action as some sort of bodily movement$_T$.

Up to this point, the argument has proceeded by thinking of actions as things we can receive more specific information about from answers to the question 'What did he do?'. (All actions are doings.) And of course any universal claim about *actions* concerns only the doings that are actions. (Not all doings are actions. 'What is he doing making all that noise?' 'He is snoring'.) I doubt whether we need to define the class of actions precisely to be in a position to assess generalizations about them, though, because we can use our understanding of 'action' (and definition can wait: see Chapter Three). Certainly our simple understanding is enough to show us that there are exceptions to a fully universal claim about actions and bodily movements. If a man carries out a long division sum in his head, or if he remains at attention on the sergeant major's orders, then there are actions, though his body can remain quite still while he does these things. But the most that I want to claim is that almost all of the things that we pick out as (intuitively) physical actions can be seen as movements of the body. That makes the thesis that actions are movements worth setting apart from various other things that have sometimes been said about actions.

3.2 Sometimes what is said is 'Actions are *mere* bodily movements'. (Cp. Davidson, 1971a, where, in apparently similar vein, he also says that *all* we ever do is move our bodies.)

It could be that the 'mere' is supposed to do nothing but add emphasis. 'Every action can be described as, merely, a bodily movement.' But if the 'mere' is not a mark of emphasis, then perhaps the claim intended is 'Every action is merely to be described as a bodily movement, all other descriptions being equivalent to bodily movement descriptions'. In that case it no longer speaks of particular actions exclusively, and we have instead a claim about our concept of action. If this claim is true, we are under a gross illusion in thinking that we can find sense in what a man does by seeing his deeds to be explicable in the light of what he thinks about what is beyond his body, and of what he wants, aspires to, holds dear, ... For seen in this light, actions can no longer be regarded as '*mere* bodily movements'. But it seems so unlikely that anyone could ever have thought that we have said all that matters about an action when we have described it as a bodily movement that this reductivist reading of 'Action is mere bodily movement' need not be taken very seriously.[6] At any rate it is poles apart from the claim about particular actions I defend.

When we find ourselves saying 'He did not merely move his finger', or 'He did something besides move his finger', we know that these may mean that there was another kind that his action was of. They no more entail that there was more than one action, or that there was some action that was not a bodily movement, than 'Frederick is something besides an animal' entails that Frederick is more than one entity. Besides being an animal, perhaps Frederick is a giraffe. And if 'Frederick is a *mere* animal' were supposed to deny that he might be a giraffe, then it would plainly be wrong.

But perhaps the point of inserting 'mere' into 'Actions are bodily movements' has been quite different. The intention may be to signal that the word 'move' is to be understood in its intransitive sense, *mere* movements being thought of as all there are when the body moves_{I}. If the difference between 'Actions are bodily movements' and 'Actions are mere bodily movements' can indeed be heard as a difference between a transitive and an intransitive 'move', then, provided that these sound like different claims, we must insist upon distinguishing $\text{movements}_{\text{T}}$ from $\text{movements}_{\text{I}}$. Although I argued that actions are $\text{movements}_{\text{T}}$ and not $\text{movements}_{\text{I}}$, I pointed out that the ambiguity in 'move' on its own could not establish straight off that any actual $\text{movings}_{\text{T}}$ are distinct from any actual $\text{movings}_{\text{I}}$. But now it seems possible that the difference in sense between the two 'move's will have application in another argument for the non-identity of a man's moving_{T} his body with his body's moving_{I}.

[6] Yet people have tried to argue to the non-identity of actions with bodily movements from the fact that our system of classifying actions is grounded in quite different interests from our system of bodily movement classification (Strawson and Warnock in Pears (ed.) (1963) especially at p. 65). Again it is said that any action performed could have been performed even if very different movements of the body had been made (Melden, 1956, pp. 530–2; Baier, 1971, p. 166); or that a bodily movement taken out of its context of action would no longer be an action (Shwayder, 1965, p. 174). How could these points show the non-identity of particular actions with particular bodily movements? They show that particulars can be variously classified, that the particulars that fall under some concept may differ from one another in various respects (cp. Davidson, 1973, p. 174), and that some individual events that fall under some concept might have been different in some respect but still have fallen under the concept.

4

4.1 Verbs like 'move', 'melt', and 'raise' have been much discussed in the linguistics literature. The problem has been to spell out the connection between transitive and intransitive, so that a good solution should tell us about the relation between persons' movements$_T$ of their bodies and their bodies' movements$_I$. There is much controversy about how a correct account should go, and controversy even about whether we should expect an exhaustive analysis of the transitive in terms of the intransitive. But details of these disputes need not detain us. For one important claim (and it is more than three hundred years old; Wilkins, 1668) has never been questioned as far as I know. Where '*a*' designates something in the category of *continuant* (rather than event), it is a necessary condition of the truth of '*a* ϕ_T-s *b*' that *a* cause *b* to ϕ_I. In that case movements$_T$ of the body are *events that cause bodily movements*$_I$. (See Appendix A for a more detailed account.)

This provides an explanation of why we do not answer the question 'What did he do?' with 'His body moved'. We can always answer with 'He moved$_T$ his body'. But that rules out giving 'His body moved$_I$' as answer, because movements$_T$ are different from movements$_T$ if they cause movements$_I$.

The explanation is perhaps surprising. Whatever events they are that cause the body to move$_T$ they presumably occur inside the body (if they can be located anywhere). But movements$_T$ cause the body to move$_I$. And actions are movements$_T$. Thus, given only the unquestioned claim of the linguists, all actions that are movements$_T$ occur inside the body.

Matters need not be different when it comes to actions that are not movements$_T$ (3.1). If we consider the trooper who stands at attention, or the man who does a sum in his head, we may find reasons other than the behaviour of the word 'move' for thinking that their actions occurred inside their bodies.[7]

It would be wrong to think that there has to be *one* place that is *the* place where an event occurs. Presumably all events happen in the world, even though many of them can be more specifically located at places that the world includes; and to say that an action occurs inside the body is not to deny (for example) that it occurs where the person

[7] For the trooper, cp. Sherrington: 'Often to refrain from an act is no less an act than to commit one, because inhibition is coequally with excitation a nervous activity' (quoted by Miller, 1978, p. 310).

whose action it is is placed. But still, I do claim that all actions occur inside the body. And that summarizes the principal thesis of this essay.

4.2 One reaction to learning that this thesis is a consequence of the linguists' claim about verbs in the class to which 'move' belongs will be to dispute the generality of their claim. The claim has been argued from examples like 'He closed_T the door (caused it to close_I)', 'He raised_T the flagpole (caused it to rise_I)', 'He broke_T the glass (caused it to break_I)'. But perhaps it cannot be carried across to cases where people do things quite directly, as they typically move_T their hands, or raise_T their arms, or open_T their mouths. It will be said that 'cause to ϕ_I' is then no longer an appropriate gloss of 'ϕ_T' (or that, if it is appropriate, this is because identity is a special and limiting case of the causal relation).

Someone who said this, and disliked the idea that words like 'move_T' and 'raise_T' always pick out actions as causings of other events, might think that we are bound to acknowledge some duality in their behaviour – that 'raise_T', for example, is true of someone who simply raises_T his right arm, but true in a different sense of someone who uses his left arm to raise_T his right. After all these are very different ways of raising the right arm. But would he also wish to claim that 'break_T' shows the same duality, because it might be true of a man and his wrist-watch in virtue of the man's pressing his arm hard down against a table (breaking the watch directly), but might be true again in virtue of his throwing it out of a tenth-storey window (breaking the watch indirectly)? These are very different ways of breaking a wrist-watch.

We should invite an opponent who asks us to contrast two ways of raising the arm to concentrate instead upon the contrast between two ways in which the arm comes to rise. Whether a man raises his right arm directly, or whether he uses his left arm to raise it (or for that matter has someone else raise it for him), there is an event of his right arm's going up. The difference between the two cases seems to be a difference in the manner in which the arm gets to rise. But if the arm's rising_I is not an event that happens uncaused when someone raises his arm directly, then is it not that he, the man whose arm rises, causes-it-to-rise-just-like-that? As Prichard once said 'By "moving our hand" we mean causing a change of place of our hand [relative to our body]' (1932, p. 19). I believe that if we can hear his remark out of the context of his extraordinary theory of willing, we may come to find it quite natural, and true.[8]

We shall have to ensure that acceptance of Prichard's claim does not commit us to the details of his theory of willing (Chapter Four), and to ensure that regarding both direct and indirect arm raisings as alike the causes of arm risings leaves room for the intuitive idea of a basic action (Chapters Five and Six). But first we need some more argument that even if someone moves his body directly, the relation between his moving_T of it and its moving_I is a genuinely causal one.

[8] Prichard spoke only of what people cause. An implicit assumption of mine has been that 'A person caused something' can be taken to say that an *event* in which the person played a role caused something. The assumption might seem to beg the question against a certain important doctrine about agency, which holds that an agent's causing an event is not to be construed in terms of one event's causing another. But I doubt in fact that I have prejudged this doctrine, because the advocates of agent causality typically speak of actions as the things that are caused by agents (Taylor, 1966, p. 127), and they do not deny that bodily movements_I are caused by events (ibid., p. 114; Chisholm, 1966, p. 19). To say that movements_T cause movements_I is to say nothing about how actions are caused, and is to leave it open whether there are events that are caused by agents alone. But if I do not contradict the claims of Chisholm and Taylor, I can wait until later to ask whether there is any problem in principle about using *event causation* to elucidate *action.* See Chapter Seven.

APPENDIX: ON GOLDMAN'S ACCOUNT OF INDIVIDUATING ACTIONS

Goldman and I are agreed that 'I did the same thing as you' and 'He did the same thing today as he did yesterday' do not record identities between particular events. He says that such sentences speak of *act types*, and that the question about individuation concerns *act tokens* (and this is exactly like my saying that they tell us that there was a *kind* of action and that what matters in individuation are *actions*). But Goldman does not think that identities between types are irrelevant to the controversy. For he believes that in order to find the identity conditions of particular actions, we need first to attend carefully to what statements about types of act say.

> [When] we say 'John signalled for a turn' . . . we ascribe an act property or [what is to say the same thing] act type to John: the property of signalling for a turn . . . . To ascribe an act type to someone is to say that he *exemplified* it. If John and Oscar perform the same act [i.e. do the same thing], they exemplify the same act type (1971, p. 769).

Goldman argues from this view of action sentences – as sentences that speak of types or properties and ascribe them to persons – to a view of nominalizations.

> Since an act token is standardly designated by a nominalized form of action sentence and since an action sentence associated with such a nominalization asserts that a person exemplifies a certain act property, it is natural to view the designatum of such a nominalization as an exemplifying of an act property by a person. Thus John's [signalling for a turn] is an exemplifying by John of the property of [signalling for a turn] (ibid., p. 770).

From the view of nominalizations, he moves to thinking that such expressions must designate events that are discriminated at least as finely as act types.

> Moreover since the act type of [signalling for a turn] is distinct from the act type of [extending his arm out of the car window], it seems natural to say that [John's] exemplifying of the act type of [signalling for a turn] is distinct from [John's] exemplifying of the act type of [extending his arm out of the car window]. (Ibid., p. 771. The

> adaptations indicated are introduced in order that a single example may be considered throughout Goldman's argument.)

Goldman holds in fact that triples of persons and times and act types determine actions. Actions are different if the agents are different, or if their times of occurrence are different, or if they are exemplifyings of different properties – whether by the same agent at the same time or not.

What leads Goldman to such a different result from mine is a disagreement about the roles of action sentences and of nominalizations. Goldman speaks of action sentences as associated with nominalizations, and nominalizations as *designating* action tokens – as if to say that each action sentence is true in virtue of some one particular specifiable action. But consider his own example of an action sentence, 'John signalled for a turn'. Even if this is actually true in virtue of John's having signalled for a turn at *t*, and even if John only ever signalled for a turn at *t*, still the sentence might have been true though John had not signalled then: it would still have been true provided that at some past time or other there was some action of John which was his signalling for a turn. The truth-conditions reveal that the sentence is existential and general: the description 'is John's signalling for a turn' can denote (*sc.* be true of) any number of actions of John, and the sentence 'He signalled for a turn' commits a speaker to the existence of at least one event that the description does denote. (Cp. Davidson, 1969b, pp. 79–81.)

Goldman's neglect of the generality in action sentences is manifest in his argument itself. At the end of the quoted passage, he concludes that John's exemplifying of the property of signalling for a turn is distinct from John's exemplifying of the property of extending the arm. 'What exemplifyings by John are these?' we might ask. Do we not need to know which particulars are in question in order to tell whether distinct particulars are in question? It is true that, so far as Goldman is concerned, it is not going to matter which particular actions he means to speak of, because he thinks that whichever exemplifying by John of signalling for a turn it is, it will be distinct from any exemplifying by John of extending the arm. But if he thinks that, then it is a general conclusion for which he should argue.

> Since the act type of signalling for a turn is distinct from the act type of extending the arm, it seems natural to say that *any* exemplifying by John of the act type of signalling for a turn is distinct

from *every* exemplifying by John of the act type of extending the arm.

This is a universally quantified version of Goldman's argument (compare the last few quoted lines). But it does not seem to be valid. One might as well reason that since the property of being author of a book is distinct from the property of being author of an article in a philosophy journal, anything that has the one property is distinct from everything that has the other property. Provided that ' – is an exemplifying by John of the property – ' and ' – has the property – ' have the same logical role, the argument about authorship exhibits the same form as the one that Goldman needs. But on the basis of the argument about authorship it should seem natural to conclude that Goldman is not Goldman.

Goldman's own claim, that John's exemplifying of *signalling for a turn* is distinct from John's exemplifying of *extending his arm*, sounds plausible because it can be taken as saying something true – that the property (of actions) of *being John's exemplifying of one property* is distinct from the property (of actions) of *being John's exemplifying of a different property*. And now Goldman appears to have traded upon the complication of introducing act properties that persons exemplify, and allowed such talk to direct our attention away from particular actions and towards *their* properties. It is when we focus on the reading of Goldman's claim at issue, in which it does not speak merely of the properties of actions, that we find it has no support from intuition. (The analogy of the last paragraph would have force even if Goldman's claim had not been recast as a general, universally quantified claim. Since Goldman believes the general claim, it can be used to make the point. It serves better to make the point because it does not have the true but irrelevant reading of Goldman's own claim; and because we need not tell a story in order to understand it: to interpret the general claim there is no need to settle upon which particular particulars are in question.)

If we wish to uncover the identity conditions of particular actions, and if we do think of them with Goldman as exemplifyings of properties, then what we must ask is when an exemplifying by a person of one property is an exemplifying by him of some other property. Goldman's answer is 'Never'. He thinks that no action can ever have more than one property that is describable as the property of being the exemplifying by a person of a certain property.

I can swiftly say why I do not find that natural by means of an example. Let it be that John moved a finger on some specified occasion. And suppose that I tell you that John's movement on that occasion attracted the barman's attention. You might think that you have now been told some more about a particular movement of John's that you already knew to be a movement of a finger. But on Goldman's view I have told you about another, different movement of John's. For *making a movement, making a movement of a finger* and *making a movement that attracted the barman's attention* are three different properties that John exemplified; and thus, for Goldman, none of the actions here is the same as any other. Suppose again that you ask me 'Which finger was the movement a movement of?'. According to Goldman you have now asked whether there was some other movement: you know that there was a movement and that there was a movement of a finger, and now you want to know whether in addition to these there was a movement of a particular finger. (Or else, perhaps, you can deduce that there was also a movement of a particular finger, and in spite of appearances it is about that that you are asking. But I wonder how you can be in a position to ask *about* that before you know *which* event it is.)

Goldman owes us an account of how 'John's movement attracted the bar man's attention' can be interpreted so as not to entail straightforwardly that there was something that attracted the barman's attention, and an account of how 'Which finger was the movement a movement of?' can be interpreted so that it is not a simple request for more detailed information about something that happened. It would be no exaggeration to say that Goldman has us using a different language when we speak about events. Familiar modes of combining words have to be understood in unfamiliar ways, common words like the relative 'that', and 'was' and 'of' come to lead a new life. The alternative assumption is that we speak the same language when we speak of events and when we speak of continuants. And a conception of events as things about which many different kinds of questions may be asked and all sorts of things told may be based upon that modest foundation.

II

BODILY MOVEMENTS AND MUSCLE CONTRACTIONS

1

It is not a novel thesis that it is our practice to describe actions in terms of their effects. But my suggestion that even when we describe actions as bodily movements we still make allusion to their effects (a suggestion I take to be the logical continuation of Davidson) has not been recognized as a consequence of our practice. Probably it has been thought that it is precisely at the point where we see actions as basic, where we think of what we do quite directly 'just like that', that we pick out the action all by itself and by reference to nothing else; at that point we cease to be concerned with any further, separate changes that the agent may have caused.

It should help one decide whether this is correct to attend to descriptions of actions that do not even get as far as the things directly done. And so we should see what happens when we go back beyond the bodily movements, when we think about actions in terms which don't reach to the surface of the body.

2

2.1 A case, familiar for the special problems it poses, makes it quite natural to speak of an agent's contracting his muscles. A man learns that certain particular muscles of his arm have to be contracted if ever he is to clench his fist; and we may imagine that he has a reason to contract those very muscles – perhaps he wants to please some experimenter. He does so. As we say: he contracts his muscles by clenching his fist.

If we say that a man contracts his muscles by clenching his fist, do we not mean that his action of fist clenching causes his muscles to contract? He cannot bring about the contraction 'directly'; he has to bring it about by way of setting himself to do something else. But the reason why fist clenching serves as the kind of action he can carry out in order that he should have those muscles contract is that actions of fist clenching cause them to contract. So it seems. But attend for a moment to the mechanism of muscular contraction. Nerve impulses cause the contractions of muscles, which in turn cause the movements we make. We have it now not only that actions of fist clenching cause muscular contractions, but also that muscular contractions cause actions of fist clenching. Even if we do not wish to rule out causal loops *a priori*, it must come as a shock to learn that we encounter the phenomenon in this commonplace situation.

Reactions to this differ. Richard Taylor takes the case to be very much as it has just been described, and finds it puzzling (1966, pp. 194-5). Von Wright discusses a similarly vexing case of someone who brings about events in his brain by raising his arm (1971, pp. 76-81). There is some contrivance by which brain events can be watched, and an observer can see that an event (of a certain type) occurs whenever the man raises his arm. Von Wright does not think that the brain events cause the arm to go up, so that the question of a causal loop does not arise for him; but he does think that we should accept that there is retroactive causation in such a case. 'By performing basic actions we bring about earlier events in our nervous systems' (ibid, p. 77). What both Taylor and von Wright are agreed on, then, is that in certain circumstances a man has some past event within his voluntary control (if only for a very short time). This conclusion alone is surely sufficiently paradoxical to make us wonder whether there has been some mistake.

2.2 My own diagnosis will occasion no surprise. Even to bring the problem to this point, I have had to suppress the distinctions made in Chapter One. But if we distinguish between transitive and intransitive uses of verbs like 'move', 'clench' and 'contract', an unproblematic account already exists.

We can begin with the homely piece of science that provides an important datum. What we know is that the muscles' contracting_I causes the fist's clenching_I; and until we have established what connection there is between the action of fist clenching_T and the fist's clenching_I, we can only say that as a result of the muscles' contraction, the fingers close_I and the fist clenches_I. But with just this much agreed, there is no pressure to deny what appeared obvious and yet appeared to make a paradox, that bringing about a muscle contraction by clenching the fist is causing that contraction to occur by clenching the fist. For such a bringing about of a contraction need not be the cause of any event earlier than itself. Although the fist's clenching_I takes place after the muscles contract_I, there is no reason to say of the action of fist clenching_T that *it* occurs after the muscles contract. Indeed, if it is right to think with the linguists of a clenching_T as cause of the clenching_I, and right to think with the physiologists of a contraction_I as cause of the clenching_I, then on ordinary principles about causation, it follows that the man's action causes the muscles to contract. But there is no backwards causation. When a man clenches his fist, this has (at least) two effects; neither of them goes beyond the body, and the first of them, the muscle contraction_I, causes the second, the clenching_I of the fist.

2.3 I conclude that we can deal adequately with the puzzle by distinguishing transitive from intransitive senses of 'clench' or 'move'. But the example will reinforce the conclusions of Chapter One in another way. It can be used to discredit the ideas (i) that bodily movements_I are identical with bodily movements_T, and (ii) that bodily movements_I are parts of bodily movements_T.

(i) An opponent of the conclusions of Chapter One who thinks that there is no real distinction between a thesis about actions as bodily movements_T and a thesis about actions as bodily movements_I may be expected to claim that a man's clenching_T his fist is the same event as the fist's clenching_I, and that his contracting_T his muscles is the same event as the muscles' contracting_I. On the view of individuation I have argued for, there is only one action when a man contracts his muscles by clenching his fist, a single performance on his part. Indeed in this case it seems more than usually obvious that having clenched his fist, there is nothing more for him to do, that no further doing is required, if he is to contract his muscles, and his feat of contracting_T the muscles is thus nothing other than his clenching_T his fist. Consider now the opponent's premise that the contracting_T = the contracting_I and that the clenching_T = the clenching_I. It follows immediately that the muscles' contracting_I is the same event as the fist's clenching_I. But this is false. (One can imagine the agent's arm wired somehow to a pointer that flickers when the muscles contract. The pointer's flicker is caused by the muscles' contracting_I, but not by the

fist's $clenching_I$. So these are events that have different effects.)
(ii) A very similar *reductio* argument is fatal to the view that 'the fist's $clenching_I$' describes a *part* of the action of clenching the fist. This view will appeal to anyone who misreads Wittgenstein's question 'What is left over when I subtract the fact that my arm goes up from the fact that I raise my arm?' (*Philosophical Investigations*, § 602). If that question is distorted in a certain manner – as if events might be a species of fact – it will seem that when we subtract the event of arm $rising_I$ from the event of arm $raising_T$, we should be left with some remainder different from either[1]. And then one may arrive at the idea that a man's $contracting_T$ his muscles is composed of his muscles' $contracting_I$, and that his fist $clenching_T$ is composed of his fist's $clenching_I$. But the man's $contracting_T$ his muscles is identical with his $clenching_T$ his fist; so his $contracting_T$ his muscles is composed of whatever his $clenching_T$ of his fist is composed of. Thus according to this new opponent, his $contracting_T$ his muscles is made up of his fist's $clenching_I$ (*inter alia*). Again the conclusion is false. The fist's clenching is not a part of his $contracting_T$ his muscles, at least if his $contracting_T$ his muscles is over by the time that his muscles have contracted.

In Chapter One, we had a stronger suggestion about the timing of a muscle $contraction_T$ – because it is cause of a $contraction_I$, it might be said to finish as the muscles start to $contract_I$. But in the argument here only a weaker and non-question-begging assumption is needed – that the muscle $contraction_T$ is over at least by the time that the muscle $contraction_I$ has occurred. (That assumption can be seen to be just, if one thinks of a contraction of the arm muscles by a man whose hand has been amputated and replaced by an inflexible block connected to the muscles. In that case there is no event later than his muscles' $contracting_I$ by which we could seek to fix the finish of his $contracting_T$ his muscles. Yet it is hard to find a convincing reason why it should make any difference to when an event of the type *$contracting_T$*

[1] Wittgenstein's actual question, unlike the question about subtracting events, does not presuppose that arm risings are parts of arm raisings. On a natural interpretation of the metaphor of subtracting facts, it presupposes rather (something half-stated in Wittgenstein's previous sentence 'When "I raise my arm", my arm goes up') that the occurrence of an event of arm rising is necessary but not sufficient for the occurrence of an event of arm raising. This presupposition is true, and the question is a proper conceptual one, even if Wittgenstein himself had doubts about it. So I argue in my 1980. In the next chapter, I give a partial answer to Wittgenstein's question. See also Chapter Nine, § 2.1.

of the muscles is complete whether or not it is the action of a man who happens to have a fist to clench.)

If actions of moving the body (of which fist clenchings$_T$ are one species) are not the same as the body's movements$_I$, and are not composed of the body's movements$_I$, then how could they be related to the body's movements$_I$ except as the behaviour of the word 'move' and the § 2.2 account of the puzzle lead us to suppose – which is as cause to effect? The drift is plain. Unless we allow that actions are distinct from movements$_I$, we cannot say how the latter are, but the former are not, caused by the contractions$_I$ of muscles. And unless we push actions right back inside the body, we cannot make good sense of talking about an action as a person's contracting$_T$ his muscles.

2.4 Because the identity I allege of (some particular) contractions$_T$ of muscles with (some particular) clenchings$_T$ of fists carries a great load in the arguments (i) and (ii) above, the problem of action individuation now appears to be crucial – especially as Irving Thalberg has recently claimed that he can describe the puzzle case convincingly by taking a different approach to individuation (1977). (I discuss his account in more general terms in the Appendix to this chapter, and also in my (1979).)

Thalberg thinks that contractions$_T$ of muscles and clenchings$_T$ of fists, though they have components such as brain events in common, differ from one another inasmuch as a clenching$_I$ of a fist is a component of a fist clenching$_T$ but not a component of a muscle contracting$_T$. His view then shares with the view rebutted at (ii) above the idea that a contracting$_I$ is a part of a contracting$_T$, and a clenching$_I$ a part of a clenching$_T$, but he can block the application of Leibniz's law and thus avoid the absurdity derived there, because he refuses to identify contractings$_T$ with clenchings$_T$.

The intuitions that gave rise to the troubles for which Thalberg and I propose rival remedies were, first, that the action of fist clenching *results in* a muscle contraction, and, second, that the action of fist clenching *results from* a muscle contraction. What I have denied is only the second: I say that it is the fist's clenching alone (clenching$_I$), not the action of fist clenching$_T$, which follows on a muscular contraction$_I$; and so far as I am concerned, there is nothing wrong with the first. Thalberg also denies the second intuition, but for a different reason. 'We have to . . . regard the tensing of your arm muscles as an event which helps constitute, rather than cause, your action of fist clenching' (1977, p. 69). But if this is his reason for denying the second, then it seems that Thalberg is obliged to deny the first intuition too. If he accepts it, then he must say that the action of fist clenching results in an event of the muscles' contracting which is finished before the whole of the action has occurred, and which causes a further event (the fist's clenching$_I$) that is another part of that same action. *a* causes *e* which in turn causes *f* where *f* is a part of *a*. That does sound like a causal loop.

Is Thalberg quite free to reject both of the intuitions that make up the puzzle? We need to rehearse the thoughts that lie behind it. A man makes it happen that his muscles contract. How does he do this? 'By clenching his fist'. So *what* he does that makes it happen that the muscles contract is clench his fist. Is this not to say that they are actions of fist clenching which make it happen that the muscles contract, which, in other words, cause them to contract? This is the train of thought that has puzzled people. But it is these thoughts that Thalberg must (and does, however inexplicitly) reject when he includes the muscle contraction$_I$ in the middle of the action of fist clenching$_T$. It seems that he has not so much redescribed and reconciled our first thoughts on the matter as simply left the troublesome ones out of account.[2]

3

3.1 How seriously do we take the puzzle about fist clenching and muscle contracting? It is not every day that a physiologist encourages us to make specific muscular movements, or that we intend to make

[2] Thalberg considers and discards a solution similar to my own when he imagines someone's saying that the problem arises out of confusing fist clenching$_T$ (making it happen that a fist clenching$_I$ occurs) with fist clenching$_I$. But implicit in his statement of this solution as he credits it to his opponent is the principle:

> If a man makes *e*-which-occurs-at-*t* happen then that man at *t* makes *e* happen. (Cp. 1977, p. 68.)

If this principle were true, then fist clenching$_T$ and fist clenching$_I$, whether or not distinct, would occur at the same time (as Thalberg assumes on p. 67). So Thalberg has forced someone who adopts my solution to find the action of fist clenching$_T$ later than the contraction of the muscles, and that is exactly what I wish to avoid. It will be clear that I reject his principle about the dates of actions.

such movements for whatever reason. It may be that the case is so exceptional that we ought not to place much faith in what we naturally take to be true of it. We start with wrong ideas about it, it will be said.

These would be damaging claims if they were right, because my own argument so far has no more plausibility than the intuitive thoughts that it frees from absurdity. But I think that the puzzle is not really special at all, and that if there is ever any problem here, there is a problem whenever a man moves his body. The case where it seems right to say 'He contracted his muscles by moving his body' simply makes vivid something that goes on all the time.

The puzzle arose at the point where we noticed that a man was contracting his muscles, and enquired how that was happening. There was reason to remark on this man's muscle contractions, because, as the case was envisaged, he had reason to make them: that was what he obligingly set out to do. But how can a man's intention to contract his muscles have any bearing on those causal and temporal relations between events which make the difficulty? When someone clenches his fist, he brings about an event of muscle contraction that occurs earlier than the clenching of the fist (ambiguity of 'clenching' deliberate: this is the puzzle). But he still brings about such an event, and it still occurs earlier than the clenching of the fist, even if he has no intention to bring such an event about. Intention seems irrelevant. And if it is, then the puzzle is quite pervasive.

Some people have thought, though, that we only do contract$_T$ our muscles, or only do bring about their contractions, if we intend to; otherwise the muscles simply contract$_I$. These philosophers make intention relevant by regarding it as a necessary condition even of having a case of muscle contraction$_T$. But then it is impossible for a man to contract his muscles until he has learned whatever it is he needs to know to be in a position to contract them intentionally. This cannot be right. If someone is taught by a physiologist how he can arrange to make certain muscles contract intentionally, then is this not to learn about what he does, to learn then about what he *did* non-intentionally before he had learned about it? (Compare: When I discover how an engine works, I learn new descriptions of what I was doing when I drove a motor car.) Of course we very seldom think of anyone's actions as muscle contractions. But then, in the normal way, our interests in someone's actions take off from our interests in his interests in acting, or else from our interests in the world beyond him which he affects. So our interests do not ordinarily concern his muscles, although they determine what we see fit to say.

All the same, von Wright and Taylor appear to have thought that there is backwards causation only where a man intends to contract his muscles. If intention to contract the muscles isn't needed to have a case of muscle contraction$_T$, then perhaps they have thought that it is needed in the argument that they give for backwards causation. But again this is a difficult position to defend. For the general conclusion that a man brings about an event in the past whenever he moves$_T$, and irrespective of his attitude to his muscles, is actually much less surprising than the restricted conclusion that Taylor and von Wright explicitly endorse – that we affect the immediate past when we act, provided that we intend our muscles to contract. If someone's having an intention to contract his muscles is what makes for backwards causation, then we must suppose that, in learning which muscles we contract, and in coming to be able to intend and by intending to execute specific muscular contractions, we come to be able to start changing the past. But then it seems as if backwards causation itself, and not just our conceiving of ourselves as exploiting it, starts with our acquisition of certain pieces of knowledge. We learn some quite ordinary things about the causation *from* the past of certain bodily movements$_T$, and then in making movements of those same sorts with their causal relata now better understood and fixed in our minds, we suddenly begin to reverse the direction of causation, *towards* the past. This is fantastic.

3.2 Finally some comment on the word 'by' as it occurs in the initial statement of the problem. 'He contracted his muscles by clenching his fist.' This 'by' has been taken to be the crux, and is emphasized in all the discussions. But if, as I maintain, the problem would arise whenever a man contracted his muscles and would arise equally whether or not he set out to do so, then either the 'by'-sentence should be true (if ever it is true) even when there is no intention to contract the muscles or else the 'by'-sentence is not really the crux. I shall argue for both these disjuncts. First, 'He contracted his muscles by moving' applies (if at all) whenever a man moves; but second, even if it never applied, that wouldn't matter.

It is not a necessary condition of the truth of 'He ϕ-d by ψ-ing' either that he intentionally ϕ-d, or that he intentionally ψ-d, or even that he either intentionally ϕ-d or intentionally ψ-d. (I deliberately lean over to reach my cup, and accidentally knock over a jug whose contents spill out. I spilt the contents by knocking it over.) This shows that there can be no direct argument from the non-intendedness of muscle contractions to the non-applicability of 'He contracted his muscles by clenching his fist'. Whatever oddity there is in saying this of someone who did not intend to contract his muscles may be presumed to derive from the predictable oddity of saying of him 'He contracted his muscles'. But truth, not naturalness, is what counts here, and we have seen reason to hold that the ordinary active man is continually contracting his muscles.

It is important to realize that the puzzle can also be stated without going through the 'by'-sentence. This helps one to see that the case for backwards causation may not depend upon the admitted peculiarities of 'by' here, but only upon fusing movements_T with movements_I, clenchings_T of the fist with the fist's clenchings_I. And anyone who denies that the peculiar 'by' sentence is ever true, and has never understood the fuss about backwards causation, will now appreciate that my own arguments do not rely upon it. (See also Chapters Five, § 4.1, and Seven § 2.2.)

He contracts his muscles. How is that? Well, he clenches his fist, and his doing so makes his forearm muscles contract. There is no use of 'by' here; but we still have an action, of clenching the fist, and something else, the muscles' contraction, that is made to happen in acting. And we can ask 'Which comes first, the action or what is made to happen?'.

Which does come first? If the action is not complete before what is made to happen occurs, then we must accept that there is retroactive causation in every case of physical action. So soon as we allow that actions of fist clenching_T carry on up to the time the fist clenches_I, we find ourselves saying that they are taking place when their effects have already occurred. The alternative is to insist that the action occurs before its consequence, and that bodily movements_T take place even before the muscles contract.

APPENDIX: ON THALBERG'S ACCOUNT OF INDIVIDUATING ACTIONS

Thalberg believes that muscle contractions$_I$ are parts of muscle contractions$_T$, and fist clenchings$_I$ parts of fist clenchings$_T$. This is one particular application of his 'component approach' to action individuation, according to which there is said to be a series of actions related as parts to wholes in any of the cases where I should say there is a single action described in terms of different effects. The matter will show up clearly in the case of Anscombe's pumper (cp. Chapter One, § 2.4). On Thalberg's view, some effect of the pumper's moving his arm added onto his moving his arm gives an action of operating the pump; some effect of his operating the pump added onto his operating of the pump gives an action of replenishing the water supply; and some further event added onto his replenishing of the water supply in its turn gives the action of poisoning the inhabitants (Thalberg, 1977, pp. 85-112, see also his (1971), and for very similar accounts, Beardsley (1975) and Jarvis Thomson (1977)). Thalberg stresses that because actions in his series overlap, they are not separate, numerically distinct things. But if I continue to ignore numerical questions, I shall not contradict this. Questions about identities come first, and, here as before, they are my sole concern (cp. my (1979)).

What made me assert an identity between the pumper's pumping and his poisoning the inhabitants was the thought that the pumper need not do anything more once he has operated the pump. And it was the thought that he must be doing something while any of his actions is occurring that made me deny that his action of poisoning the inhabitants could carry on any longer than his operating of the pump. Since Thalberg thinks that the action of poisoning continues well beyond his operating of the pump, either he must give up the idea that an agent has to be doing something for the duration of any of his actions, or else he must allow that an agent may be doing something after he has ceased to be active. (Remember that the pumper could have died after his arm left the pump, but still have poisoned the inhabitants; and that similar counterfactuals can often be constructed.)

Thalberg hopes to avoid this dilemma by regarding actions as a sort of thing that can 'take on broader dimensions with time' (1977, pp. 110-11). If we can conceive of an action becoming longer – not continuing simply, but actually acquiring its own temporal parts – then in the problematic cases we shall have first an agent who does something, and his action (his doing that thing) will then be prolonged despite the fact that he has ceased to do anything. But can we coherently conceive of this? I believe we shall see that we cannot, if we try to press Thalberg to say *which* is the action that takes on new parts as time progresses. What does the pumper do, his doing of which is supposed to carry on after he has done that thing?

Thalberg cannot answer *operate the pump*, because he holds that the action of operating the pump does not go on after the pumper's hand has left the pumping mechanism, so that we have here an action of which we can say that it occurs when the agent is doing something, but not that *it* continues afterwards. Again Thalberg cannot answer *poison the inhabitants*, because he holds that the action of poisoning does not take place until the inhabitants have drunk the poisoned water, so that we have here an action of which we can say that it continues after the agent stops doing anything, but not that *it* acquires a part before then. It is the operating of the pump to which a part is supposed to be added to obtain the poisoning; but the operating of the pump is different from the poisoning according to Thalberg.

Evidently the difficulty here is quite general. How could there be an action that is both an action a, and also – what its acquisition of a part would require – a different action $a + e$?

We could escape from the difficulty, and restore the principle that actions are doings of things by agents that occur when they do those things, only if we identified the operating with the poisoning. Thalberg himself sometimes speaks as if such actions were the same (e.g. at 1977, pp. 116–17). But if he really does wish to turn to my view of identities, then he must abandon the component approach. For if he were to say that the operating of the pump o both causes further effects e and is identical with events $o + e$ that have those further effects as parts, then he would have it that o not only finishes when o finishes, but also (if o really is the same as any event $o + e$) finishes when any of its effects e does. And it would be a mad view of action from which we could deduce that actions always cease when agents stop doing things, but also keep on finishing at later times, as their more and more remote effects are complete.

Thalberg wanted to say that there are actions that are composed both from agent's doings of things and from events that are not agents' doings of things. And his problem is to find any event about which both of these things could be true. There is a correlative problem for him – of explaining how the things that are true of actions could be true about any event.

Thalberg agrees that many of the descriptions of actions we employ pick them out in terms of things that they cause. For example, he concedes the claim that any killing that is an action is an action that causes a death (ibid., p. 101-2). In a particular case, we might know more than this about a killing – say, that it was a *shooting* that caused a death. And we might know more about the shooting – most likely it was *a movement of a finger against a trigger.* So we can say of the killing that it was *a movement of a finger against a trigger that caused a death*. Construing the relative clause 'that caused a death' as relative clauses have to be construed, we have here a complex description of a movement ('it is a movement x, such that . . . x, and x caused a death', as we say). But this way of understanding the English description is not open to Thalberg. He agrees that the movement that caused a death is a killing; but he denies that the killing is a movement, because, according to him, every killing, but no movement, has a death as a part of it. Thalberg then has to hold that the description 'movement that caused a death' does not apply to any movement, and certainly not to any movement that can be said to have caused a death.

Goldman, too, was unable to recognize action descriptions as built up from their component linguistic parts. For Goldman the problem is quite ubiquitous, because he thinks that no two action descriptions (unless they ascribe the very same property) can be descriptions of the same thing. Thalberg's conception of events is very different from this (1978), and since he would assert many identities that Goldman would deny, the problem for him is not as widespread. None the less, in any of those cases where Thalberg would deny identities that I should assert – wherever we describe actions by way of their causal relata –, he can make no more sense of what we say than Goldman can.

In many discussions of action identities, there is a presumption that all of the parties are agreed about what actions are, and all would be talking about the same things, but that somehow in any particular case a dispute has emerged over whether the same thing is being talked about. It is as if Goldman and Thalberg and Davidson all shared a conception of events, and that Goldman chose to discriminate them finely, Davidson coarsely, and that Thalberg, a trimmer, elected to compromise. This picture of the controversy has prompted one recent writer to say that 'perhaps no position on these matters is "the" correct one', even if in practice we have to pick one view and talk as if it were correct (Davis, 1979, p. 41). But if we believe that, in speaking about what people do, we talk about actions, and that what we say about actions is true or false according to how actions are, then the only possible view is the one that makes the same sense as we make in narrating what is done. The philosophy of action does not need to invent or to stipulate its subject matter.

III

ACTING AND TRYING TO ACT

1

We began with descriptions of actions that have been taken (for certain purposes) to be the basic ones – *bodily movements*$_T$ –, and saw grounds for locating actions further back in time than the overt movements$_I$ of the body. Then we turned to descriptions of actions in (causally speaking) even more basic terms – *contractions*$_T$ *of muscles* –, and found that we cannot make space for these, unless actions are 'right inside the body'. The trail from bodily movements back to muscle contractions may be followed further. We can ask whether there are descriptions of actions so basic that they are free of any specific commitment to consequences like the body's movings$_I$ or the muscles' contractings$_I$. Is there any type of event instances of which can be shown to occur before the muscles contract, and instances of which can be shown to be actions?

I shall answer these questions 'Yes' in this chapter. Every action is an event of *trying* or attempting to act, and every attempt that is an action precedes and causes a contraction$_I$ of muscles and a movement$_I$ of the body.

The chief thing that the sceptical will require me to establish is that the province of *trying* can be as large as this implies. My view is that occasions on which a man tries to do something are not only some of the occasions on which in trying to do something he succeeds in doing something else. For first, we try to act in a certain way whenever we intentionally act in that way (§ 2.1 and § 2.2); and second, we may try to act though there is no action at all (§ 3.2). The first point suggests that every action is accompanied by a trying. The second will help to demonstrate that at least some tryings do not reach to the surface of the body. But if that can be shown to be true of all tryings (§ 3.3), then, if actions may be identified with the tryings that accompany them (§ 2.3), we shall reach the general conclusion that actions themselves lie within the body (§ 4).

2

2.1 It seems that it is only appropriate for a speaker to say that an agent tried to ϕ, if, for some reason or other, the agent did not – or it was thought that he did not – straightforwardly and easily ϕ. Perhaps the agent needed to exert himself specially in order to ϕ, or perhaps, through bad luck or bad judgment, he failed to ϕ; in such cases it may well be said that he tried to ϕ. In Grice's idiom, there is a disjunctive set of doubt or denial ('D-or-D') conditions – here of doubt whether or denial that the agent succeeded –, and a speaker who says 'He tried to ϕ' will normally be taken to hold that one of the conditions in the set is fulfilled (Grice, 1961). But 'the fulfilment of the relevant D-or-D condition is not a condition of either the truth or the falsity of a statement [to the effect that someone tried. It is only that] if this condition is not fulfilled, the utterance of a statement [that says that he tried] may well be extremely misleading in its implication.' (I adapt here one of Grice's claims about perception, p. 139, to make my claim about action.)

If this is right, then the province of trying can extend much wider than would be supposed by someone who was content with asking when we should normally have cause to say that someone tried. It can be argued that it spreads very wide indeed. So far from failure or its possibility providing a necessary condition of trying, success gives a sufficient condition: we try to do everything which we intentionally do. (For the substance of the argument, I am indebted to Brian O' Shaughnessy (1974). I endeavour to formulate a quite general version.)

One can imagine an onlooker who has excellent grounds for thinking that a certain agent has every incentive to do a certain thing, but who also has excellent grounds for thinking that the agent will not succeed. The onlooker knows moreover that the reasons he has for thinking that the agent will not succeed have never been brought to the agent's attention. In the particular case, his belief that the agent will fail to do what he wants, though justified, is false. In fact the agent straightforwardly does what he had an incentive to do. Then, on the basis of his knowing of the agent's reasons, and of his knowing that the agent thought there was no obstacle, the onlooker is surely right if he says that he knew the agent would *try* to do it. So the agent did try.

The onlooker might, for example, know that a friend of his thinks there is treasure hidden under a boulder in the garden. The onlooker does not suppose that his friend will succeed in shifting the boulder, because he has been told that the boulder is much too heavy for his friend to move. But he has been misinformed. In the event, the friend simply and effortlessly rolls the boulder to one side. The onlooker admits that he was mistaken. But he says 'I was right about one thing at least. I knew that my friend would try to move it.'

What such examples bring to light is this: the kind of doubt or denial that in the ordinary way makes it appropriate to speak of trying need not impinge upon the agent himself, and thus need not affect whether it is true that he tried. It was only the onlooker who had any doubts that his friend would move the boulder, and the friend did not exert himself specially. But then, recognizing that we can tell a story which leaves everything where it was for the agent, and yet which shows that it is obviously true to say that the agent tried to act, we may come to see that agents do try to ϕ in every case where they set out to ϕ and succeed in ϕ-ing.

The critical step in the argument is the step from 'None of those things that went on outside the agent and that prompted the spectator to say that the agent tried impinged upon the agent' to 'Therefore even if these things had not gone on, the agent would still have tried'. Can we be sure that the spectator's doubts, or the grounds for them, really make no difference to whether the agent tried? After all, it can make all the difference to whether you know that p whether it is true that p; and whether or not you count as knowing that p can also be affected simply by whether others have found reason to doubt that p. (cp. Harman, 1973, p. 146). Might not the question whether an agent *tried* also depend upon how things were outside himself, or upon how they were thought to be?

Now there is one perfectly good sense in which what a man tries to do does depend upon how he and the world are related. Whether someone is now trying to learn a Shakesperian sonnet, for instance, may depend upon whether it is a Shakesperian sonnet that he is now trying to learn by heart – a question he may be misinformed or have no particular views about. But this creates no general problem, because there is no need to assume that the agent's states of mind are given exhaustively in the premises of the argument. We can insist that the question how the agent's action is to be characterized should always be settled at the start of any particular use of the argument; and, provided that it contains a true description of the agent's action which can properly be used in stating both what the agent knows he has reason to do and also the onlooker's belief about the agent's reasons, the argument will proceed.

There would be a genuine threat to the argument if someone could show that, in circumstances where both A and B know that A intends to ϕ, an uncommunicated doubt on the part of B as to whether A will actually ϕ in itself affects the question whether A will try to ϕ. But however plausible something analogous to this may be in the case of knowledge, there is nothing to support it in the case of trying. And if that is right, the critical step is unobjectionable.

2.2 There may be doubts about the scope of the argument. If it is to be seen to establish anything general about action, then evidently we must say which pieces of human behaviour count as actions. We observed that there are fewer actions than there are events that can be mentioned in answering the question 'What did he do?' (Chapter One, § 3.1); but we need now to state explicitly what the extra condition is of something's being an action beyond its being someone's doing something.

I take over Davidson's claim that all and only actions have descriptions under which they are intentional (1971a) (with a caveat to be entered below, n. at § 3.3). This characterization explains our view of the cases in Chapter One. We do not say that a person who snores *acts*, because there is no description of the event of his making the sounds he makes that can be used to tell us of anything he intentionally does. We readily allow that the trooper who stood at attention and the man who did sums in his head both behaved as *agents*, because we do not have far to go to find values of ϕ such that 'He ϕ-d intentionally' is true of them: very likely the trooper stood at attention intentionally, and the man did his sums intentionally. So we have support for the idea, which Davidson defends much more amply, that if we go through a list of things that were done when there was someone's action – a catalogue of the different kinds that subsume this action of his –, then we shall find at least one thing in the list such that we can truly say '*He did that intentionally*'[1].

Granted this, the argument about trying can be applied (potentially at least) to every action, provided it need only be assumed that the agent intentionally did what he had incentive to do. And nothing more than that is needed. It doesn't have to be taken for granted that the agent *forms* an intention to act, or that he has the thought of his action at the front of his mind. Consider Brown who has a daily routine of waking up, getting dressed . . . , which he carries out habitually, without reflection or ado. One day someone is provided with a reason to think that Brown ate something on the previous night that causes specific motor disturbances, and to think that as a result Brown will not be able to knot his tie this morning. Brown none the less is unaffected, and carries out his routine absolutely as normal, knotting his tie in his usual unthinking way. The person who knew what he had eaten is surprised to learn that Brown had done this. But he always knew that he would *try* to knot his tie.

Of course we cannot always invent examples that show it would be natural to say that people have tried to act. But anyone who thought that that was an objection to the argument would be missing its point. It is not claimed that whenever anyone does anything intentionally, we could imagine someone else on the scene who could say with all propriety 'He tries to do that thing'. It is rather that, by way of seeing that we can often envisage a person in that position, we should be persuaded (defeasibly perhaps) that 'He tried to ϕ' is not merely compatible with a man's success in ϕ-ing, but integral to his having ϕ-d

[1] Someone might retort that the most interesting question about any doing is whether it can show anything at all about a person's psychological states; and then he might say that a serious concept of action should include in its domain *senseless* actions such as tapping the feet or the fingers, or rattling the keys in one's pocket for no apparent reason. We take such activities to reflect a person's states of mind, though they are not carried out intentionally (O' Shaughnessy, 1974; Locke, 1974). To this the reply can only be that it is doubtful whether we can straightforwardly effect any cut-off between movements which do and movements which do not have a psychological history (cp. Williams, 1978, p. 284), and that we have to draw boundaries where we can find significant boundaries to draw. If we take an interest in regarding ourselves as rational creatures much of whose behaviour receives a satisfying explanation when it is seen to issue from our beliefs, and desires, interests and concerns, then the restriction of actions to events that can be characterized in such a way that we can see that something was intentionally done when they occurred will enable us to deal with a vast area that we take to matter. (Cp. Chapter Six, § 2.1.)

intentionally. The examples help us to recognize (the analogue of what Grice recognized for perception) that what makes it true of someone that he tries to ϕ has nothing to do with whether ϕ-ing is difficult for him, or with whether he thinks that it may be difficult for him. What makes it true that he tries to ϕ has little to do with his attitudes – except in so far as his having those attitudes actually brings it about that he does something, which, if there is no difficulty, is to ϕ.

2.3 What is it though to try to act in some way?

Sometimes it is to act in some other way. Jane tries to return a service at tennis, and hits the ball into the net. One thing she did was try to hit the ball, and another thing she did was hit it into the net. But it is not that one has to do first the one thing and then the other in such cases, that having tried to hit the ball over the net (having had a shot at it), one then has to mitigate one's failure to get it over the net by now hitting it into the net. Having attempted ineptly to hit the ball over the net, one has already done all that one needs to do to have hit it into the net. One's trying to return it *is* one's hitting it into the net.

It seems that matters cannot be otherwise if one succeeds in doing exactly what was attempted. If someone's trying to hit the ball somewhere can be the same as his hitting it elsewhere, then his actually hitting it where he meant to could scarcely be different from his trying to hit it there. One thing that is done then is try to ϕ, and another thing that is done is ϕ. But having made a movement that is an attempt at ϕ-ing, no further doing is called for from the agent if he is to have ϕ-d. His attempt is then a success.

This recalls Chapter One (§ 2.4). And indeed the arguments given there are bound to commit us to believing in identities between tryings and actions – to accepting that attempts may be successes – because among the verbs from which more complex verbs can be made in construction with 'by' are verbs that result from embedding in the context 'try –'. 'He knocked the picture off the wall by trying to straighten it.' 'He tried to turn on the light by flicking the switch.'

Suppose that John does try to turn on the light by flicking the switch, but that the bulb has gone. A spectator who knew that the bulb had gone and who disbelieved that John would succeed in turning on the light may have known that John, in his ignorance, would at least try to turn it on. He could take his flicking the switch as proof that he tried to turn it on. And it seems that he has his proof because John's switch flicking was his trying to turn on the light. But if (by § 2.1) flicking the switch was something else that John tried to do, and yet John did not make two attempts at getting the light on, then there was only one (variously describable) trying on his part. Thus his switch flicking must equally be his trying to flick the switch. His succeeding in ϕ-ing is his trying to ϕ.

2.4 If ever we ϕ intentionally, then we try to ϕ (§ 2.1); if ever we try to ϕ and succeed in ϕ-ing, then our trying is our succeeding (§ 2.3). Thus, provided that every action of anyone is his intentionally doing something (§ 2.2), it is the same as some trying. At this point all that is needed for the conclusion that no action includes an overt bodily movement$_I$ is that no trying includes an overt bodily movement$_I$. (More would be needed for a complete account of the relations between attempts and actions; see Chapter Six, § 2.1 and n.2. Note now that nothing here shows that we always intentionally try-to-act.)

3

3.1 Some philosophers have thought that we cannot speak of trying where merely moving the body is in question, that 'He tried to ——' does not make its ordinary sense unless '——' is filled by a description of an action that is non-basic (Davidson, 1971a, p. 24; Danto, 1966, p. 58). But one of these philosophers has an argument that a man may both try to ϕ and succeed in ϕ-ing which suits me very well.

> I dial Jones's number . . . If I fail to reach Jones, I say I will try again, meaning that I will again dial that number, and if I reach Jones, I will have succeeded, even though *I* did nothing differently on that occasion than on the one before (Danto, 1966, p. 57).

Thus we can say that at the second attempt, when I try again to reach Jones, my attempt is my reaching him. But similarly we could argue that someone's second attempt to move his body might be his moving his body. If a man has a disorder in virtue of which he suffers intermittently from partial paralysis, he may try to move his arm and fail, and say that he will try to move it later. Then when he tries, he may succeed.

The Gricean argument also can be applied to the case of bodily movement. Indeed since that argument provides us with a quite general strategy for showing that one who intentionally ϕ-s may also try to ϕ, it makes it difficult to deny that move the body is something one can try to do. But still, any purported proof of that will have at least to acknowledge the possibility that a person should try to move his body and fail to move it. And probably it is this possibility that has seemed so hard to credit.

3.2 Hume did not think that it needed arguing that we can fail in attempts to move our bodies. In discussing knowledge of causation, he used this example:

> A man, suddenly struck with a palsy in the leg or arm, or who had newly lost those members, frequently endeavours, at first, to move them, and employ them in their usual offices (*Enquiry*, Sect. 7, pt 1).

Another useful example is Landry's patient, mentioned by William James. He had lost all sensation in one arm, and when he was asked to put the affected arm on top of his head with his eyes closed, he could do so if he wasn't prevented. But when he was prevented, when, unknown to him, his arm was held down, he was surprised to find upon opening his eyes that no movement had taken place. Again it seems that he tried in vain to move a part of his body (James, at p. 490 of vol. II of [1950] edn). (Silber (1964) reports that the phenomenon is found also in non-diseased subjects whose fingers have been anaesthetized.)

These natural statements of what goes on in the two examples have met with much resistance, however.

About the first, it has been said that we tend to think that a man with the palsy tries to move his leg only because we conceive of him learning of his paralysis through this little piece of reasoning: 'I try to move my leg, it doesn't move; therefore, I cannot move it' (cp. R. Taylor, 1966, pp. 77-85). But we surely do better to suppose that the man's knowledge that he cannot move his leg is direct and non-inferential: what he learns is that he cannot move it, and that he is not in a position even to try to move it now. Some people hold that this latter description gives a complete account of the man who discovers he is paralysed, because (they say) we do not really have any conception of what a pure trying without outward and visible signs would be. A man who claims he is trying to wiggle his ears simply will not be believed unless there is some external manifestation of his efforts.

All of the power of this objection may be derived from our reluctance to suppose that one will try to do what one *knows* to be impossible. We interpret a man's action by seeing it as his doing something that he had some motive to do. We know that he wants to ϕ, that his movements can be construed as his ϕ-ing, and then sometimes we know why he is doing what he is doing. But this style of interpretation will make sense of a person only if we are prepared to add that he does not think that ϕ-ing is something he cannot do. For, even if we know that a man wants to ϕ, if we also think that he thinks that there is no way that he will ϕ, then we can expect his desire to be to that extent inert. Where he lacks the relevant belief, then, we shall usually have no reason to think that he will try to ϕ, and (unless we know that he has a motive for trying to ϕ that is additional to any motive he might have for ϕ-ing[2]) we shall have a reason to think that he will not try to ϕ. That will explain why we are apt to disbelieve those who would claim that they are trying to wiggle their ears: most of us know whether we are able to do this or not. It would explain, too, why we soon cease to think that a man whose leg has become paralysed can go on trying to move it: at some point he will surely have learnt that it is impossible. But the man who concerns us is someone who discovers that a part of him is unexpectedly paralysed. *Ex hypothesi*, he has no knowledge of the impossibility at the time.

Landry's patient certainly did not realize that it had been made impossible for him to move his arm. He was surprised on occasion to find that he had failed to move it. And here it has to be explained not only that he believes (if he does believe it) that he has tried, but also that he believes that he has succeeded. The patient did not suppose that he had moved his arm except on those occasions where he has been asked to move it. On those occasions where he was asked to move it, and also, unknown to him, was prevented from moving it, no movement$_I$ would explain his belief, and the supposition that he tried to move his arm seems to be inescapable if we want to make any sense of the episode. There is no question that he learns of his failure by inference from his having tried. It is rather that unless *we* say of him that he tried, we cannot see why he should think he succeeded. We cannot understand why he should be curious to know exactly what went on when he finds out that his arm has not moved.

[2] All the examples I have met of someone's trying to do what he knows to be impossible are examples of a person who has a reason to try to ϕ that persists even if any reason he has for ϕ-ing is eliminated. (Sometimes we lose face if we aren't seen to make an effort, for example.) See e.g. Williams, 1978, p. 172, and Thalberg, 1962 (though Thalberg's examples are cited as examples of *intending* the known impossible which may be more problematic).

But there is a line of objection directed specifically against the case of the patient. It will be said that his reaction is best explained by supposing not that he tried but that he *acted*. He is an authority on what he does; and so, since he believes that he has done whatever he does when he actually moves his arm, he must have done whatever he does when he moves his arm. It has even been suggested that we should say 'So far as he, or the mental side of him, but not necessarily his arm, is concerned, he moved his arm' (Vesey, 1961, pp. 363, 364. Davis also thinks that there is an action; 1979, p. 41, n. 16).

One of the remarks made in objection to the first case can be turned to advantage here. If an agent really were authoritative about when he had acted, and could know that he had moved his arm so far as the mental side of him was concerned, then why are we not always inclined to think that, whenever people claim pokerfaced to be trying to wiggle their ears, they must be doing something – to wit, wiggling their ears as far as the mental side of them is concerned? But they are not. And it seems equally obvious that the man who discovered that his leg was paralysed cannot be said to have done anything. He discovered precisely that he could not do what he wanted.

But there is one difference between the two cases which might seem to affect the question whether the patient who had lost sensation in his arm acted. Didn't he, unlike the man with the recently paralysed leg, show some signs of trying? Wasn't some force needed to prevent his arm from rising? Or perhaps there were contractions of muscles that could have been detected with suitable equipment. And if there was nothing of this sort, then working with normal assumptions about what it takes to move an arm, we shall suspect that the patient really did not try. (We do not feel this about the newly paralysed man, because we take paralysis to act high up in the nervous system.) This is all true. But it must be remembered that the patient intended to do no more than move his arm. He did not set out to tense it, or to contract his muscles. Of course if the muscles do contract, that will be excellent evidence that he has tried to move his arm. But unless his arm also moves_I, there is no evidence that he moved_T it. Even if all actions are tryings, not all tryings are actions.

3.3 It is significant that it would alter things to change the last example slightly, by supposing that the patient was someone who had learnt that he could contract certain muscles by moving his arm, and that his intention was to contract those muscles. Then, provided only that they contracted$_{\mathrm{I}}$, we would, I think, say that there was an action. He did what he set out to do.[3]

And now it seems that there could be an event that was actually not an action, but that might have been an action. If the patient whose muscles contracted when he was prevented from moving his arm had set out to contract those muscles, then nothing that went on inside him beyond a certain point would need to have been different in any way. Certainly he wouldn't have done anything differently, because he would have known that all he needed to do in order to contract his muscles was to move his arm. So if only the unintended consequences of his trying to move his arm had been intended, the event of his trying would have been his doing something intentionally, an action of contracting the muscles.

Further thoughts of this kind will explain what temptation there is to say that the patient who did not move his arm nevertheless acted. We feel that if the patient was surprised that his arm had not moved, then there must have occurred something exactly like what would have occurred if his arm had moved. But if we allow that there is an event of the patient's trying, then certainly there is an event of the same kind whether his arm moves or not. Not only that: we may also think that the very event that occurred when his arm did not move might have been a moving$_{\mathrm{T}}$ of his arm. If only his arm had not been prevented from moving$_{\mathrm{I}}$, it would have moved$_{\mathrm{I}}$, and then his trying to move it would have been an action of moving$_{\mathrm{T}}$ the arm. (The distinction

[3] This contrast, between the case where he meant his muscles to contract and the case where he did not, provides nice support for Davidson's idea that something intentionally done is required for action. But we must modify Davidson's criterion of action now that we have seen that, in special cases, someone may try to do something without also doing any of the things that he tried to do. The problem is that it seems possible that in at least some such cases the patient *intentionally tries to move his arm*. But if that is so, then we have an answer to the question 'What did he do?' which cites something that he did intentionally, although we do not have an action. Call *simplex* any description of a doing which does not contain any other description of a doing embedded in the context 'try to ——'. Then actions are all and only the events that have simplex descriptions under which they are intentional.

(Perhaps there is a sense of 'do something' (DO something) in which trying to do something is never DOING anything. If that were right, then we could stick to Davidson's formulation, taking over this sense of 'do'. Note, however, that treating *his trying to ——* as a species of *his doing something* (§ 2.3 above) relies only upon a fact about ordinary usage, that 'He tried to ϕ' sometimes does give an appropriate answer to 'What did he do?')

between concepts of action and particular actions, of which so much was made in Chapter One, is paralleled here by a distinction between what is essential to *movement*$_T$ and what is essential to particular events that are potentially movements$_T$.)

We can also understand why one should be inclined to think that an agent is authoritative about whether he acts. There are types of events – trying to act in certain ways – with respect to the occurrence of which the agent may have a certain authority, and instances of such types may be actions. This is to say that there are events that the agent is particularly well placed to know about, and that some of them are actions. But it is not to say that an agent always knows, or knows better than anyone else does, whether he has acted. For in order to be actions such events must result in bodily movements$_I$ (or in contractions of muscles, if they are all that the agent tries to produce); and the agent need not have any special authority whether bodily movements$_I$ have occurred, as the sensationless patient shows. (Of course kinaesthetic sensations, which are missing for Landry's patient, will in more ordinary circumstances put the agent in a peculiar epistemic position with respect to the results of his attempts to move his body. I discuss knowledge of action in Chapter Eight.)

Some of this is speculation. But even if it is wrong to hold to the strong claim that particular tryings that are not actions could, except for the impediments, have been tryings that are actions, the weaker claim I need, which the speculation does something to support, is that attempts to move the body that are not successes have very much the same status as attempts to move the body that succeed. This is certainly true of people's attempts to turn on lights: these may be flickings of switches, movings of fingers, tryings to flick switches . . . whether or are not they are successful. Why should matters be different in the case of attempts to move the body, which, if they fail, have no overt effects? What leads some people to think that even unsuccessful attempts to move the body are actions should rather make one think that, as with all other attempts, the principal difference between the successful and unsuccessful sort is that the unsuccessful ones do not have the intended effects.

4

4.1 If there is an action that is someone's intentionally moving his body, then that someone tries to move his body (§ 2.1 and § 3.1). Moreover his trying to move it is his moving it (§ 2.3). Trying to move the body if it is not an action is an internal event, possibly with external signs (§ 3.2). But it need make little difference to trying events *per se* whether or not they are actions (§ 3.3). So the tryings that are actions are also internal events.

Stated in this general way, the argument applies only to actions that are intentional-described-as-bodily-movements; and it is not obvious that all actions have this property (and may be false, see Chapter Six, § 3.1). Nevertheless, if the argument can be carried through for particular instances of a wide range of action kinds (and it can), then at least it will show that some actions from a wide range of kinds are internal events. It would be strange, though, if some but not all actions of any kind were internal events. And again it would be strange if actions of very many kinds were internal events and yet not all actions were.

It may help to appreciate the cogency of a general claim to review the underlying strategy of the argument. Take an action describable in various ways – as a ϕ-ing, as a ψ-ing, as a χ-ing . . . . Under some of these descriptions under which it is intentional it will be redescribable again as a trying to act in that way – a trying to ϕ, a trying to ψ . . . . (There may also be further descriptions of it as a trying – if the agent was unsuccessful on some score.) Next, we can often construct examples to make it clear that for some one description in the series of action descriptions, and for some one description in the series of descriptions of tryings, the action is to be identified with the trying. (Trying to turn on a light was flicking a switch.) But then, in any particular case, however the action is described as an action and however the action is described as a trying, we can affirm an identity. It remains only to show that it is clear for tryings as they are described in some way that they are always internal events. This is made clear for trying to move the body.

4.2 The first two chapters purported to show that actions are causes of bodily movements$_I$, this chapter (*inter alia*) that actions are tryings to move$_T$ the body or bring about bodily movements$_I$. Together the claims entail that, where successful, trying to move the body is causing it to move$_I$. If that has any independent merit, then the argument from causing reinforces the argument from trying, and vice versa. But the argument from trying gives us an independent route to the conclusion that actions are internal events.

IV

ABERRATIONS OF VOLITIONALISTS

1

It is a familiar line of criticism against certain doctrines about action that they import mysterious mental entities into an account of what it is to act, and that this involves them in a regress and commits them to an untenable dualism. I need to show that my thesis that actions are tryings is immune from any such criticism.

Everything here will hinge upon a distinction between two sorts of views about actions. A view that holds that actions are *caused* by volitions is very different from any view which says that actions are to be *identified* with items of some (apparently) mental type.

Locke stands as representative of the view that volitions cause actions, and I doubt that he can escape the familiar criticisms (§ 4.1). But so far from my account's sharing the mysterious and dualistic features of Locke's (§ 4.2), it actually precludes them (§ 4.3). Much the same goes for Prichard's account (§ 5). For Prichard does not claim that volitions cause actions, and his is a theory of the same general shape as my own, even if, as he presents it, it displays some of the same mysteries as Locke's.

I have to establish in the next two sections how very different from one another theories like Locke's and Prichard's are (§ 2). For although they are very different, they are liable to be confused with one another (§ 3).

2

2.1. One very straightforward difference between the account I have given and some traditional volitionalist accounts is evident. No mention has been made here of any such items as volitions[a], acts of will[b], wills[c], willings[d], setting oneself to act[e], undertaking[f], decisions[g], or thoughts[h]; and only the notion of *trying* serves the arguments of the previous chapter. (These terms are used by the following authors: (a) Hobbes, Reid, Locke, Berkeley, Hume, Mill, Austin (the jurist), Sellars (1966), Davis (1979); (b) Descartes, Hobbes, Locke, Hume, Bentham; (c) Hume, Austin, Bentham; (d) Locke, Hume, Davis (1979); (e) Prichard (1932); (f) Chisholm; (g) Binkley (1976); (h) Locke, Prichard (1945), McCann (1974), Foley (1977).)

This is a significant difference, because the technical uses of volitionalists have provoked much of the criticism of the position. The critics have asked: 'What is the substance of the claim that a man willed, if it cannot be explained what this means by pointing to ordinary cases where it is obvious that the term applies?'; or 'Why is it that only philosophers have to talk of acts of will or of setting oneself to act, if these things are really essential to action?' *Tryings* are at an advantage here. 'Try' is a common enough word. And at least there is no problem about showing that people sometimes try to act, even if it takes a philosopher to find a serious interest in showing that when we act we always try to act.

Still, it might be wrong to make too much of this terminological difference. Fashions in vocabulary change, and recognizing this, someone might say that tryings are just willings by another name. I deny that tryings are at all the same as willings. But I need to speak to people who have thought that they can knock down with one salvo every account that introduces 'mental' events of any sort as concomitants of actions (cp. Ryle, Wittgenstein and Richard Taylor). It will help in considering their charges, if, at the outset, we ignore the fact that different items are postulated in different accounts, and select a word that is neutral between different doctrines. For the time being, let us follow William Hamilton (1870) who used 'conation' as a generic term. We can think of *conations* as covering any of the more specific *willings, volitions, acts of will, settings of oneself to act, tryings,* etc., which have figured in particular accounts. Beliefs and desires will not be counted as species of conations. But it will not be treated as a necessary condition of being a conationist that one take conations to be the operations of some distinctive faculty of The Will. The characterization has to be left as unspecific as this, because, if I am right, it will emerge that no single definitive thesis is held by all of those who have incurred criticism for introducing mental items into the elucidation of action. (It follows that the use of 'conation' is a semi-technical one. But it is brought in here to organize a controversy, not to state any particular theory.)

2.2 Those who have believed that conations exist have not all agreed even about what role such things play. One must distinguish in the first place between the thesis that conations are the same as actions, and the thesis that they are causes of actions. This distinction marks the most conspicuous difference between the view I favour and the standard empiricist accounts of Locke and Hume. Philosophers whom I follow in the view that conations are actions include Berkeley, Prichard, and possibly Descartes. (For Descartes see e.g. *Letter to Arnauld 29 July 1648,* § 4, at p. 235 in (1970).)

In the second place, the empiricist view that conations are causes of actions admits in its turn of two variants. It may be said that the events that are causes of actions are actions, or this may be denied. That conations are events that simply cause actions is what seems to be most consistently held by Hobbes, Locke, Reid, Bentham, Hume, and, recently, by Sellars. The view that conations are both causings of actions and themselves actions may not be very popular; and even though talk of *acts* of will suggests this view, it is hard to find an explicit and unequivocal expression of it anywhere. (Hobbes, *Leviathan* Part I, Ch. 6, in (1968) p. 127; Reid, *Essays Concerning the Active Powers of the Human Mind* Essay IV, Ch. 8, in (1969) p. 56, 60, 221; Bentham, *Introduction to the Principles of Morals and Legislation* Ch. VII, § § 13–15, in (1970) pp. 76–8; Sellars, 1966, 1976.)

This tri-partite classification – conations as actions but not causes of actions; conations as causes of actions but not actions; conations as actions *and* causes of actions – is not exhaustive. Mill, for instance, held that conations were parts of actions, the other parts being movements$_I$. '[An action is] not one thing, but a series of two things: the state of mind called a volition followed by an effect' (*Logic* 1.iii.5). But even if the classification is too gross to include all possible views, or to register all the subtleties of particular views, the three kinds of account that it admits are well worth distinguishing.

2.3 A consideration of Ryle's famous regress objection points sharply to the differences. The objection starts with the assumption that the philospher under attack takes the occurrence of conations to distinguish between 'mere bodily movements' and the voluntary movements that are actions. It is said then that a conation, in order to serve the role it is meant to play, must itself be a voluntary action. But, according to the conationist, to be a voluntary action a thing must be caused by a conation. So there must for each conation be another. But then for any action there must be an infinite series of different actions. And that is absurd (Ryle, 1949, at p. 65 in (1970)).

This *reductio* tells at most against an account that identifies conations both with causes of actions and with actions themselves. For the fundamental step is: whenever there is one action, there are two actions; and the conclusion is: there are infinitely many actions. But anyone who takes either of the other views distinguished does not believe that whenever there is one action there are two, and the objection does no damage to him. Someone like Locke or Hume, who holds the plain causal view of conations, might simply deny that a conation needs to be caused by a further conation in order for the status of voluntary action to be conferred upon its effect. And someone like Berkeley or Prichard or me can reply to Ryle that a conation is always the same as an action, so that again there is no question of its needing to be caused by any other conation.

No doubt neither of these two replies to Ryle tells the whole story. Ryle himself endeavoured to block the first reply for Locke and Hume by posing his argument as a dilemma, of which the regress argument constituted only one horn. And Prichard, to whom the second reply would have been available, believed that the account from which that reply arose carried with it the danger of another regress, akin to the Rylean one. But the point to notice here is that the first reply seems to have found much more favour than the second. Many people have remarked that conations might be used to mark off actions without being counted as actions themselves (e.g. Warnock, 1963, p. 19; Kenny, 1976, p. 26; Danto, 1973, p. 54); whereas the other response – that a conation may not need to play the role of causing actions – is never considered. Since this other reply seems to be quite as effective as the first, and since some of those who have the reply at hand have been thought to be vulnerable to a regress argument, there is cause to wonder why it should have been neglected.

I think that the main reason for the neglect is that the two views that give rise to the different replies are so easily confused with one another. If the confusion between them leads to their conflation, then that would explain why at most one of the views has seemed worth defending, and why only one reply has been noticed. The possibility of confusing the two views would also explain why the regress argument has been thought to be as powerful as it has been thought to be. For the argument is powerful precisely against an account that combines features of both views; and a confusion between two views can lead to their contamination. The first view is that conations cause actions; the second view is that conations are actions; and the account that the regress argument undermines says that conations both cause actions and are actions.

No one is likely to be happy about my siding with Berkeley and Prichard, unless he is aware of some of the interrelated sources of confusion here. Each of the first four parts of the next section will draw attention to some mode of confusion between two kinds of role that conations may be meant to play. Having set these forth, I shall be better placed to argue against the account of Locke, and to rescue what truth there was in the much despised account that Prichard gave. Ryle was indeed right to accuse some volitionalists of regressive accounts, but for Prichard there was no need to worry that his theory led to a regress.

3

3.1 Some scholars have seen it as the central task of a philosophical account of action to separate actions from 'mere bodily movements'. As Melden put it:

> It appears as though an action were a bodily movement of a special sort and that we only need to specify the distinctive features of bodily movements that count as actions in order to elucidate the concept of action (1956, p. 523).

If this is how one regards the problem, then it is natural to suggest that the distinguishing feature of actions will concern their causal history, and that the distinction between what is caused by some sort of conation and what is caused by something 'outside one's control' will separate actions from other movements.

But of course there is ambiguity in this line of thought. Is 'movements' here being used transitively or intransitively? If it is used intransitively, then the problem of distinguishing actions from other bodily movements is misconceived. No action is the same as a movement$_I$

of the body – a mere $moving_I$ of the hand, say. So a distinction between actions and $movements_I$ is not a distinction to be drawn within some class of events. The other possibility is that 'movement' is to be taken in its transitive sense in the statement of the problem. Although that would achieve the contrast between actions and other movements that is needed to set the problem up, the proposed solution may not then seem so compelling – at least if it was inspired by the thought that the difference between actions and other movements must have to do with different ways in which the body is immediately caused to $move_I$.

This is not to deny that there may be some manner of stating the difference between actions and other $movements_T$ in terms of causal history. (Perhaps actions alone are related in some way to beliefs and desires.) The point is that among the causes of bodily $movements_I$ are actions, and that that must be borne in mind by someone who wishes to propose a volitional antecedent in order to give an explanation of how the body comes to move when we act. If he states that $movements_I$ are caused by conations, then he need not be saying anything about the causation of actions.

We see that Hume may have vacillated between the two different views of the status of his conations (volitions or willings) in the following pair of quotations. In the first, they are apparently said to cause $movements_I$; in the second, $movements_T$.

> The will being here consider'd as *a cause*, has no more a discoverable connexion with its *effects* than any material cause has with its proper effect. So far from perceiving the connexion betwixt *an act of volition*, and *a motion of the body*; 'tis allow'd that no effect is more inexplicable from the powers of thought and matter (*Appendix* to *Treatise* for Bk I, Pt 3, § 14; my italics).

> A will [= a willing] . . . is only the cause from which an action is deriv'd (*Treatise*, Bk III, Pt 1, § 1)

Someone may start by conceiving of conations as the things by means of which we cause our bodies to move – as causes of motions of our bodies ($movements_I$). From there it does not follow that conations cause actions. But if one forgets the ambiguity in 'move', it is easy then to slide into thinking that conations do cause actions ($movements_T$). In that way one can shift from the unproblematic doctrine – that conations (tryings) are identical with actions – to the utterly different doctrine which I take to be the official doctrine of Locke and of Hume – that they cause actions.

3.2 Berkeley's claims about action have often been criticized alongside those of Locke and Hume. But Berkeley's conations are not the causes of actions. He asks rhetorically 'Can you conceive of any action besides volition?', and thinks that volitions are nothing other than actions. What they cause are motions. But 'motion is a sensible quality and consequently it is no action' (*Second Dialogue Between Hylas and Philonous*, at p. 217 in (1949), vol. II). There are no two ways about it in Berkeley's view, and the confusion this time is in the minds of his critics.

Jonathan Bennett says that we may treat Berkeley's claims about voluntary action as an analysis of

'*X* did *A* for a reason, or intentionally, or deliberately';

and that the analysis Berkeley offered was

'*A* occurred because *X* performed a volition' (1971, p. 207).

Berkeley's thought is well represented by this, provided that we understand '*A*' in the *analysans* to stand for a motion of the body. Then we have Berkeley saying such things as '*X*'s finger moved because he performed a volition'; and this is perfectly correct, because Berkeley thought that we do things in virtue of our volitions' causing motions of our bodies. The trouble comes when we look back to the *analysandum*, and try to make sense of it in the same way. No action is the motion of a finger. We do not do our finger's movings$_I$, and nor did Berkeley think that we do. (Of course we do not 'do our movings$_T$ of our fingers' either. But that shows that there is a mix up of particular events with kinds of events in addition to the blunder that concerns me here; cp. Chapter One, § 2.2.)

If we read Bennett's schema consistently, and take the notion to be analysed to be action and take the 'because' in the analysis to be causal, then we must attribute to Berkeley the claim that actions are the upshots of a species of conation. So the schema misleads us into counting the items that are the effects of actions as actions themselves. Bennett is not the only philosopher to have used the schema. And I suspect that he is not the only philosopher to have allowed its use to lead to an assimilation of two very different views about conations. (Bennett's basic criticism is that Berkeley's view leads to the conclusion that we never do anything. Although I reject Bennett's interpretation, I think he is right in that. But this is because of an internal difficulty in Berkeley's metaphysical scheme of things, and not because of his account of action taken by itself.)

3.3 The third source of error that I wish to bring to notice can be exposed by considering these sentences:

He caused himself to raise his arm (his raising of his arm),

He caused his bringing about the explosion,

and

He caused his arm to rise (his arm's rising),

He caused the explosion.

The first two sentences tell us about him and his action, and say that he caused it; the second pair tell us of a causal relation between him and some other event, an event that is the effect of his action.

Time and again in reading philosophy about action, one finds it said (if not always so explicitly) that people cause, or bring about, their actions. Danto once wrote 'Most of the things that we cause to happen . . . are actions'; and even someone who invites us to observe the ambiguity in 'move' has written 'It seems plain that . . . when an agent raises his arm, he brings about those events which cause his arm to rise' (Montmarquet, 1978, p. 139). But if we look carefully at the sentences above, we shall see that what we ordinarily say that people cause are not actions at all, and thus that we do not ordinarily say that people bring about those events (at any rate not all of those events) that cause movements_I. Rather we say that people cause, or bring about, the events that result from actions, like explosions or the risings of their arms. Philosophical talk of causing actions, like the talk of doing x, springs from all of the exigencies of achieving a generality that we ordinarily have no need to achieve. But our common speech suggests that this philosophical talk is strictly inaccurate, in which case it fails to achieve any correct generalization.

In Chapter Seven I shall argue that only rather rarely do we cause our own actions. For the present all I claim is that we most certainly do cause their effects and that this is not the same as causing actions themselves. If we confuse our causing actions with our causing their effects, then in turn we shall confuse causes of actions with causes of effects of actions. But that may be to confuse the causes of actions with actions, and to mistake the volitions of Locke and of Hume for the (so-called) volitions of Berkeley or the tryings of my account.

3.4 Each of the previous three passages has had to do with something that may go wrong before conations are even introduced on the scene. But it will now be necessary to think about the conations themselves, and to stop supposing that all of the various species are quite alike.

Bentham noted the distinction we need to appreciate. As he put it 'The intention or will may regard either of two objects: 1. The act itself: or 2. Its consequences' (*Introduction to the Principles of Morals and Legislation*, Ch. 8, § 2; at p. 84 in (1970)). Now at least in present-day non-philosophical English, the usual grammatical construction with 'will' requires us to say 'He wills the card to move (that the card $move_I$)', and not normally 'He wills to move the card (that he $move_T$ the card)'.[1] That is, if conations are *wills*, then (as we speak now) their objects are the consequences of acts and not acts themselves – $movements_I$, not $movements_T$. But it is otherwise with other conationist verbs. We say 'I try to move the card', and never 'I try the card to move', and the objects of *tryings* are actions and not their consequences. We need to distinguish between two kinds of conation – according as their objects are actions or their consequences; and we may expect it to make a difference to the status of items of each kind what objects they regard.

The difference can be grasped by considering this account of empiricist theories of volitions:

> [A] theory begins by asserting that there is a class of conscious occurrences which are, or express, propositional attitudes, and the members of this class have the following property: each has a tendency to cause an event which satisfies or fulfils its propositional content (Goldman, 1976, p. 68).

Suppose that a volition is a willing, say someone's willing a teaspoon to bend. For such a volition to have (as Goldman says) 'a tendency to cause events which satisfy its content' is for it to be such as to cause a teaspoon to bend. Since a teaspoon's bending is not an action, the causal model of volitions may be appropriate here, but volitions of this sort will never be causes of actions. Suppose on the other hand that the

[1] In the eighteenth century both constructions may have been available with 'will', as they both still are with 'intend'. A justification for the bracketed 'that'-paraphrases may be got from examining a wide range of verbs that take the two sorts of construction. But there is a superficial explanation of the occurrence of 'the card' before the verb in 'He wills the card to move' and after the verb in 'He tries to move the card'. An explanation is given by saying that normal English word order is preserved in both of these infinitival constructions, but that where the verb is transitive the subject is deleted.

items for Goldman's theorist are tryings to act. The propositional content of a trying is (that there be) an action. But now the causal account of the relation between volitions and their contents will not be appropriate. Someone's trying to bend a teaspoon may cause the teaspoon to bend, but if it does, then, most likely, it is his action of bending the teaspoon. So it would be accurate to say that tryings have a tendency to *be* events that satisfy their propositional contents, or to cause events in virtue of which their contents are satisfied; but such volitions do not cause events that satisfy their contents.

(If Goldman has stated the empiricist account correctly, he may unwittingly have brought to light a difficulty in it. Willings cause events that satisfy their contents, but do not thereby cause actions; tryings do not cause events that satisfy their contents, although their contents are actions. But neither way does a conation have the property that Goldman credits to volitions *and* the property of causing actions. Until some new volitional verb is found, then, Goldman's empiricist's volitions cannot be the causes of actions. Yet causes of actions are what the empiricists [Berkeley excepted] seem to say that their volitions are.)

We observe once again how easy it can be to misapprehend the role of conations. Someone has only to make a faulty transition between the different kinds of content of different kinds of conation, and he will come to think of events that are the effects of actions (the contents of one kind of conation) as if they were actions themselves (contents of the other kind).

3.5 'Conations are actions'. 'Conations cause actions'. These sound like two very different theories. But if one states either theory using the language of *movements* (§ 3.1) or of *doing x* (§ 3.2), or if one states either theory in terms of things that people cause (§ 3.3) or of conations of some unspecified sort causing events of some unspecified sort (§ 3.4), then they may not sound like different theories at all. This shows that one or other of the two theories may well have come in for objections that it does not deserve. What I have to do next is to take a theory of each sort in turn, in order to show that all of the stock objections should rightly be amassed against one theory.

4

4.1 Locke insisted that agency belongs to a person and not to his body (see *Second Reply to Stillingfleet* (1812) vol. IV, pp. 301–24). To insist on that might seem to protect him from at least one of the confusions we have noted. For a contrast between events in which a person crucially and centrally participates and events in which his body participates might be a contrast between movements$_T$ and movements$_I$. How then did Locke arrive at his particular volitional account?[2]

If the person acts and the body moves, as Locke thought, then one may ask 'How does the person get his body to move when he acts?'. It is easy to scoff at this question as out of place. But Locke had his reasons for asking it. He saw that a man's desires cannot be the end of the causal story leading up to the movement of his body, and he wanted to know more about the predecessors of movements (*Essay*, II, xxi, 30 and 40).

Suppose that you want to move your finger and that your finger moves. Since wanting moves nothing, something must invervene between your wanting and your finger's moving. What is the intervening thing? How does your finger come to move? A dualist will put this problem in his own way: something of a certain sort goes on in the mind, and then there is a bodily event; what bridges the gap between the two? But we can avoid the dualist's formulation and continue to be puzzled how a movement of a finger can spring straight from a desire.

Locke proposes volitional items as the intermediaries between mind and motion: 'By a thought directing the motion of my finger I can make it move when it was at rest' (*Essay*, II, xxi, 21). He has different names for his intermediaries: sometimes *volitions*, sometimes *preferences*, sometimes *thoughts.* But whatever name they go by, their introduction constitutes no advance with the problem of how a person makes his body move. The idea that someone's body should move just because he thought that it would, or preferred it to, or willed it to move, is no less baffling than the idea that a desire should move his body. A man who knows he has become paralysed may be able to think as well as anyone else of his body's moving, and he can will as hard as

[2] It may force on writers a certain determinacy not always present in their works to ask them questions cast in the terms of an explicit event language. Of course there is no unequivocal statement in Locke of the thesis about events that I extract from him. (But it does seem to be true of Locke, and not of Berkeley, that when he says that his volitions are actions, he is recording their act-like quality, and not asserting an identity between them and 'physical' actions.) I feel more sure that others have believed that Locke held the view that volitions cause actions than that we can say for certain that it was his view.

he likes that it move. Thought or willing alone is not what brought about movements when he could make them. If you simply think of your body's moving, or will that it move, nothing happens.

If the inefficacy of desires prompts the postulation of willings, then the inefficacy of willing may be expected to lead to the postulation of some other kind of item between mind and body. And now the objection of regress comes into its own. Volitions must have a certain status to do the job for which they are intended. But if they were given that status, then we should need to pile volition on volition in order to explain any action.

At this point it may be said that it is a mistake to expect philosophical enquiry to find the immediate causes of bodily movements. Perhaps it is the place of the scientist to discover those causes; or perhaps they must remain forever a mystery (as Locke suggests at II, xxiii, 28). But do we not know often how a man's finger came to move? Wherever he acted, there is at least one incontrovertible answer to the question 'Why did his finger move?' – 'Because he moved it' (cp. Brown, 1968, p. 48). What is more we may know that he moved it because he wanted to do exactly that. Does not this bridge the causal gap between the desire and the bodily movement? Something does intervene between the two – it is an action of moving_T the finger.

This has seemed too obvious. But perhaps we can understand why the question 'How does a man get his finger to move?' should have seemed worth pressing. If we attend to the moving_I of a finger, an event that starts as it were at the knuckle, then there is nothing wrong with asking how it comes about, and quite reasonable to think that we should not be stuck for an answer in non-scientific terms. It is when we shift to the distinct question how we move_T our fingers that there is a difficulty. And for this we may legitimately turn to scientific investigation (see Chapter Six). But if we fail to realize that the two questions are separate, then we may take it that a single answer is needed for both and be unable to see where to look for one – unless we are tempted to introduce Lockean volitions.

The dualist thinks of an item that is physical – a finger's moving –, and of an item that is mental if anything is – a desire to move the finger; and then the space between the two needs filling in. Or he may think of his mind as the repository of thoughts and wants and may identify himself with his mind, so that he can no longer take it at face value that he (himself) moves his body. That seems to have been Locke's mistake. He saw that a person's acting is different from his body's moving, but was never prepared to follow through the thought that it might be his moving his body.

Of course it is an absolutely familiar complaint against dualism that we have no idea how causation might operate from immaterial mind to material body. But as the difficulty presents itself in the case of action, it can be put in this way: By making a clear separation between the mental states and the physical motions, the dualist can find no room for actions themselves.

4.2 The problem with *willings* was that they do not move the body. There is no such problem about *tryings*. Try to move your finger, and it will move (unless you are so misled by the instruction that you forget to try). This difference is one we should predict if events of trying that have the right effects are actions, and actions are movements$_T$, and movements$_T$ are proximate causes of movements$_I$.

In one respect, however, tryings are not fit for the role that Locke thought that volitions should play. For Locke assured his readers that we simply find it in ourselves that our soul may think, will and operate directly upon our bodies (II, xxi, 15 and xxiii, 20); but we do not find it in ourselves that we try to act (unless this means that on the basis of philosophical reflection we may come to see that it is true of ourselves as it is of everyone else that whenever we act there is something we are trying to achieve). Perhaps, though, Locke credited his volitions with some phenomenal character only because he knew no other way to persuade us of their existence. If so, tryings are again at an advantage over willings as candidates for the universal accompaniments of actions. We have no need to think of them as conscious occurrences in order to believe in them; and we know what is true of them without concocting a special theory.

4.3 The argument that has led me to identify every action with some trying to act was free from dualistic assumptions. Nor is dualism a consequence of that identification. Even as we endorse the claims about trying, we move away from the difficulties of the Lockean account.

If we think of our actions as the causes of our bodily movements, we seem bound to think of them as the same as the physical things which we know to cause the body to move. But then, when we think of our actions as tryings, the path to finding any further item to act on the physical is blocked. Locke and Descartes thought that the first term in a causal chain that is otherwise physical is a purely mental thing. But the identity of actions with tryings suggests that no first term is required anterior to the admittedly physical thing.

Any dualist who wants to introduce a purely mental item into my account of action would need to look back beyond the trying (which is the action, and is something we know is physical). To make his case he must postulate a further something responsible for initiating the entire physical chain. Suppose then that there is such a volition as well as an event of trying, and that this results in an event that causes the body to move – an event in the brain. Perhaps the dualist will want to say that its content is to be given as a volition that *a certain sort of brain event occur.* But our brains are not parts of us that we can move at will, and we have no idea how to make events in the brain occur as the result of such volitions as this. (Cp. Williams: 'If the Cartesian account is correct . . . the only part of my body directly responsive to my will is one which I cannot move at will' (1978), pp. 289-90.)

Another idea the dualist might have is that the content of the volition is that *the trying be effective*, e.g. I will that *my trying to move my arm result in a movement of my arm.* But again this does not seem to be something that I *can* will. For it is in no sense up to me which events cause which other events (as Wittgenstein might have meant in saying 'The world is independent of my will' *Tractatus*, 6. 373).

There is a third thing for the dualist to say about his extra, mental volition, and this is that it has the very same content as the trying. But if it does, then it has no role to play. If movings_T cause movings_I, and tryings to move_T are movings_T, then events that occur in the brain are already sufficient to start the series that finishes in a bodily movement_I.

At this point, anyone bent upon showing that dualistic volitions can be combined with what I claim for trying must resort to saying one of two things: either that the effects of actions are overdetermined – that even when we know of a physical event that suffices for the chain of physical events, we can still say that the chain has another cause, which is a mental cause; or that the extra volition there is besides the trying does not engage causally with the physical events. An immediate difficulty for each of these hypotheses is that it seems impossible to say how one could distinguish it from the other hypothesis. They do not say the same; but what would it be to know something that served to show which of them was right?

The conclusion must be that a theory that identifies actions with tryings has no need to posit anything more than physical events. If anyone should try to convert the theory into a dualist theory, at best he will be adding redundant items.

5

5.1 Prichard rejects the common view that to act is 'to originate or bring about some not yet existing state of affairs'. He says that this is something 'we ordinarily think', but that it is at fault nevertheless (1932: at p. 19 in (1949)). Even more oddly, he conceives of willing as 'an activity whose nature we are dimly aware of in acting', and which we can become 'more clearly aware of . . . in reflecting on ourselves' (1945, p. 189).

This sounds very like the position I have argued against, and utterly different from anything that could be supported by my own arguments. But if we examine Prichard's account, we shall find that it has an affinity with my own, that his arguments need not force anyone into the denial of common sense or the bizarre conception of willing, and that it is instructive to disentangle the mistakes that led Prichard to such excesses (mistakes that are still made; n. 3 below).

Prichard relies principally on a distinction between direct and indirect bringing about. He thinks that a good answer to the question 'How did *a* ϕ?' where ϕ-ing was bringing something about *indirectly*, will take the form of specifying something that *a* brought about more directly than what he brought about in ϕ-ing. For example, 'How did Jones cure his headache?' – 'He took aspirins, and the taking of aspirins caused his headache to be cured.' But if we turn to something *directly* brought about and ask how it was done, e.g.

> 'How did I move my hand?', then this cannot mean 'By causing what did I cause it?' . . . because *ex hypothesi* I am not thinking of the action as one in which I caused some particular thing by causing something else. The legitimate question is 'What was the activity by performing which I caused my hand to move?' and an answer would be 'Willing the existence of the movement' . . . what I called moving my hand really consisted in setting myself to move it (1932, p. 32).

Prichard is right when he recognizes that 'my moving my hand', just like 'my curing my headache', imports the idea of something's having been caused. (He gave a very accurate account of verbs like 'move$_T$'

(1945), p. 191.) And he is right also to see that the force of our intuition that hand movings are 'direct' is that typically we cannot answer *How*?-questions addressed to them by finding some other item more immediately caused than them, in our causing of which the hand is thought of as having been moved. The point is that we are unable to conceive of the action of hand moving in terms that mention items causally prior to the hand's moving at the same time as including in our conception of that action something that the agent meant to cause to occur. This shows that if we try to think about how a hand was moved, and find ourselves thinking of something before the hand's moving, it may prove we are thinking of something that might not have had any corporeal effect at all.

From this, Prichard drew three connected but distinguishable conclusions. (1) There must be some way to think and speak about actions without making reference to their effects; (2) introspection will show us the way; and (3) introspection will thereby reveal the true nature of action. But none of these things follows from Prichard's initial claims.

(1) For all that Prichard said, it might have been that actions were things we always describe in terms of their effects, and that our understanding of *action* did not supply us with any answer to the question what an action is except for an answer that tells of what it brought about. We do not think that there needs to be any property shared by every cause of any explosion – except that all such events cause explosions. But that does not lead us to doubt that there are events that cause explosions about which we can coherently talk.

(2) Even if we were persuaded that all movings$_T$ of the body must of necessity share something (else) in common, there would still be no reason to believe that looking inwards on ourselves should be the route to discerning the common property.

(3) Even if we did think that, through introspection, we can find some non-causal characteristic common to all actions, there would still be no reason to say that what we then discovered was the whole truth about actions. Prichard seems to have supposed that once we stop characterizing a moving of a hand as a moving of a hand, and start to conceive of it instead as an activity inside us, we should suddenly attain a true view of its nature. 'What I called moving my hand *really* consisted in setting myself to move it', he says (my emphasis). But why do descriptions of actions as willings (or as tryings) have to displace their descriptions as hand movings? Realizing that the things

that are actions might not have to be described as the bringings about of changes, Prichard claimed that we should give up thinking that acting is bringing about change. The mistake is to think that in arriving at a new conception of actions we have to abandon an old one.

Someone who comes to be persuaded that actions are tryings will steer clear of Prichard's mistakes. For the arguments that lead to an identification of actions with tryings do not start with any presumption that some effect-free identification must be possible. Asking in a spirit of agnostic enquiry whether there is some way to talk generally about actions without commitments to effects of certain kinds, no one is likely to be tempted to think that, having characterized an action as a trying, it is then open to him to think of it as something with *no* effects at all.

5.2 The very name that Prichard eventually gave to his own brand of conation must alert us to the possibility that he introduced them in default of finding anything else to play a part that he supposed he had some obligation to find some items or other to play. Given its sense and the history of its use, 'willing' would seem to be a good term only for things that *cause* actions (if it is good for any things). The typical volitionalist takes actions to issue from the objects of the Will. And we must expect that some spurious consideration is influencing anyone who identifies actions with either willings or volitions.[3]

[3] Berkeley had his own reasons for calling actions volitions. But we find the claim that actions are volitions or willings in some modern writers, such as Foley (1977), McCann (1974) and Davis (1979).

Foley arrives there from two assumptions, (i) that a person who ineffectually attempts psychokinesis is correctly described as willing something, and (ii) that the difference between ordinary action and vain psychokinesis resides in the fact that action has the willed effects.

McCann employs a disguised version of the logical connexion argument, which is one route to Prichard's conclusion (1) above. (A crude version goes: movements$_T$ cannot merely be causes of movements$_I$, because movements$_T$ are 'logically connected' to movements$_I$. So we must call them volitions or thoughts.)

Davis follows a different path to Prichard's (1). He thinks that the functionalist needs to characterize a class of events that might as well be called volitions. But we have seen that his technical use of 'volition' is not innocuous. When Davis legislates that the occurrence of a volition/willing/trying is always sufficient for an action (cp. Chapter Three, 3.2), he allows the stipulations he makes about volitions to rebound on matters that ought not to be the subject of stipulation. We may wonder what purpose could be served by the assertion that actions are the same as some items picked out by a term whose use must, if the assertion is not to be false, be a purely technical use. (One might as well say that actions are actions.)

5.3 Prichard had a particular reason for choosing 'willing' to name the items that he identified with actions. He thought that certain versions of the view that actions are conations are unacceptable. If to will is to act, and to will is to will an action, then, he supposed, to will must be to will the willing of an action; and he judged accordingly that what we will are movements$_I$ and not actions (1945, p. 192). (I imagine that it was the fear of regress that prompted him to change his terminology from 'setting oneself' in 1932 to 'willing' in 1945. The objects of 'setting oneself to' are actions, but the objects of willing may perfectly well be movements$_I$.)

Where Ryle had an argument to show that conations cannot both be actions and causes of actions, here Prichard claims to have an argument to show that actions cannot both be actions and the objects of conations. We could add this pair of arguments to our catalogue of sources of confusion between items that cause and items that are actions (in § 3). For they are easily mixed up by anyone who supposes that the connections between conations and the events mentioned in specifying their contents has to be a causal one. At any rate, we should examine Prichard's argument now. By exposing its invalidity, we shall locate one more force that took him from his unexceptionable premises to his extravagantly strange conclusion, and we shall end the chapter where it began, by quashing a charge of regress.

Prichard's argument may be stated for the case of 'try'. Since an action of ϕ-ing is an event of trying to ϕ, someone's trying to ϕ must be his trying to try to ϕ. But again, his trying to try to ϕ, if the content of a trying is an action, must be his trying to try to try to ϕ . . . .

It appears that the truth of 'Anything which is a ϕ-ing is a trying to ϕ' is used in this argument to guarantee the replacement of 'ϕ' with 'try to ϕ' in the context 'try to –'. But compare the claim that, in the presence of 'Anything which is an F is a G', 'F' can be replaced with 'G' in the context 'not –'. The result is that we may conclude from 'Not F*x*' that 'Not G*x*', i.e. that we have licensed the fallacy of Denying the Antecedent. The onus is on the user of Prichard's argument to justify his step.

If the argument is meant to rely on intersubstitution, then some sort of equivalence between the intersubstituends will be needed. If 'try to —' were a plain extensional context, and if 'ϕ' and 'try to ϕ' were coextensive, then there might be a valid argument. But since some tryings to ϕ are not ϕ-ings, such predicates are not in general coextensive. In any case 'try to –' is not extensional, but an opaque context, so that even if there are instances of 'ϕ' such that 'is a ϕ-ing' and 'is a trying to ϕ' have the same extension, there is still no valid intersubstitution even in the particular case.

Given the opacity of 'try', anyone defending the argument will look for some principle about *trying* to assist it. He may say that necessarily if anyone tries to ϕ, then provided that he knows that 'ϕ-ing' and 'ψ-ing' are in some respect equivalent, he must also try to ψ. And then any philosopher (if there be any) who holds to some equivalence between 'ϕ-ing' and 'trying to ϕ' will be committed to saying at least of himself who knows this equivalence that he tries to try . . . to try to ϕ whenever he ϕ-s. But there is nothing to recommend this principle, let alone the imaginary philosopher's states of mind. Take the equivalent pair 'run' and 'satisfy the French predicate "court" '. It does not seem right to say that anyone who knows that these are equivalent and who tries to run tries to satisfy the French predicate 'court'.

The principle that if one knows that all ϕ-ings are ψ-ings and tries to ϕ, then one tries to ψ would evidently be more useful to an advocate of Prichard's argument. Some people accept something similar about knowledge:

> If one knows that all ϕ-ings are ψ-ings and knows that there is a ϕ-ing, then one knows that there is a ψ-ing;

and they might think that we get something true if we replace 'knows that there is a ϕ-ing (ψ-ing)' in this principle with 'tries to ϕ (ψ)'. But (a) the principle about knowledge derives from the assumption that people always 'put together' the pieces of knowledge they have, and that is in general false, and (b) the principle for 'tries' is problematic in an additional respect. We seldom try to do what we want not to do, but we may find ourselves knowingly doing something that we want not to do, being aware that we have to do it in order to achieve something that we are prepared to try to achieve. A man might know that he was unable to please John without upsetting Mary, that all pleasings of John by him are upsettings of Mary by him. But he might try to please John without trying to upset Mary.

This last point shows that something positive can be said against the supposition that my claims about *trying* lead to a regress.[4] We

[4] Gregory McCulloch, whom I thank for encouraging me to make these last arguments plainer, has suggested that anyone out to show that my own claims lead to a regress will argue:

normally do not try to do what we think we have no reason to do. But when we know that we can ϕ and have a reason for ϕ-ing, though this reason may prompt us to ϕ (and so, if I am right, to try to ϕ), it need not supply us with any *reason* to try to ϕ. In that case why *should* we try to try to ϕ?

If a tries to ϕ, then try-to-ϕ is something a does.
But if anything is something someone does, then he tries to do that thing.
So a tries to try to ϕ.

Now the premise used here is not one that I adhere to, unless 'something someone *intentionally* does' is meant in the antecedent. But:
(i) There are now no general grounds for thinking that the argument works even for the single step shown here, unless there are general grounds for thinking that whenever there is an action someone *intentionally*-tries-to-do-something.
(ii) To demonstrate that this argument leads to a regress, it would need to be proved that whatever anyone tries to do, he intentionally tries to do *that*. And this is the principle my last paragraph above is directed against. (The argument of Chapter Three that took us from 'is a's ϕ-ing intentionally' to 'is a's trying to ϕ' has no tendency to take us also to 'is a's intentionally trying to ϕ'. Indeed one of the things that that argument discloses is that it may be true that someone tried, even where *because he did NOT intentionally try* it is not natural to say that he tried.)
(iii) My argument for the principle 'If he ϕ-s intentionally, then he tries to ϕ' assumed implicitly that the values of ϕ concerned are not descriptions of a form that already contain the word 'try'. So it is possible that the principle relating 'ϕ intentionally' with 'try to ϕ' is correct at most where 'ϕ' is replaced by a simplex description of an action (see note 3 to Chapter Three, § 3.3). If so, then the single step of the argument – purporting to show that we try to try to ϕ – will not be justified even in the special case where *a intentionally* tries to ϕ.

V

BASIC ACTION AND CAUSATION

1

Prichard began his arguments with a conception of things that we do directly. But he seems to have abandoned that conception in saying that only willings are actions proper. Many people will think that he was wrong to abandon it, that he captured in the idea of things directly done the concept of a basic action, and that the distinction between what is basic and what is non-basic is so deeply rooted in our thought about action that it must be preserved. And then a critic may wonder whether it can be preserved on my own view, given what I say about trying.

On my view there must indeed be some respect in which trying to move the hand is more basic than what we say is done directly, so that hand movings$_T$ are in some sense less than basic. I also agree with the critic that there is something significant in the idea of what we do quite directly. But both points will be accommodated, provided that we distinguish (at least) two different ideas of basicness. This suggestion is not a new one; others have said that there are various ideas of basicness that need to be kept separate (e.g. Baier, 1971).

In this chapter I shall attempt to define a causal notion of basicness, and in the next a teleological one. In part this is a dialectical project: I hope to show that the distinction between these two notions is perfectly natural and lends support to what I have already said. But I engage in the project also because I think that to take further the idea of what is directly done will reveal something important about the way that agents conceive of their place in the world. That will arise from the teleologically basic. But the causally basic is where the discussion of basic action began.

2

2.1 Danto was the first to give an account of the term 'basic action'. He thought that there had to be some basic actions if there were to be any actions at all. In its most general form, his idea can perhaps be put in this way: some actions depend upon others for their occurrence, but not every action can be so dependent upon another one. Danto himself believed that the cardinal dependence between actions was of a causal kind. He said:

> (1) B is a *basic action* of x if and only if (i) B is an action, and (ii) whenever x performs B, there is no other action A performed by x such that B is caused by A.
>
> (2) B is a *nonbasic action* of x if there is some action A performed by x, such that B is caused by A.
>
> (1963, pp. 435-6, his lettering adjusted.)

Now it follows from this definition that every action of x is either a basic one, or else an event in a causal chain, some earlier link of which is also some action of x. If a person moves his finger, flicks the switch, turns on the light and illuminates the room, then we should conceive of his moving his finger, his flicking the switch, his turning on the light, . . . as different actions, each the cause of its successor. This obviously conflicts with the account of action individuation defended in Chapter One, which says that as we proceed through the series that runs from his moving$_{\mathrm{T}}$ his finger to his illuminating the room we describe and re-describe a single action in terms of less and less direct effects. Certainly descriptions like 'the finger's moving$_{\mathrm{I}}$', 'the switch's going down', 'the light's going on' (etc.) can denote causally related items: but none of these is a description of an *action*.

Even if the account of individuation is in dispute, it is now agreed on all hands that the quoted definitions are unsatisfactory for the kinds of case they were supposed to deal with (Stoutland, 1968; Brand, 1968; Goldman, 1970; Danto, 1973; Pears, 1975). The trouble is that a man's doing one thing does not, as Danto suggests, generally *cause* his doing another. There are some cases where actions of x cause distinct actions of x. I might cause myself (intentionally or unintentionally) to write a letter to a friend by summoning up an image of him; and my summoning up the image then causes my writing the letter. But I do not cause myself (either intentionally or unintentionally) to turn on the light by flicking the switch when I simply flick the switch and turn on the light. Anyone who holds that my flicking the switch and my turning on the light are two separate actions, and who wants to mimic Danto's definitions, will need to define some new relation between these things (cp. Goldman's *causal generation* (1970, p. 22–5)). But if he believes that the action of flicking of the switch is the same as the action of turning on the light, then he will need to replace the idea that one action is dependent upon or more basic than another with the idea that an action's having one property or description may depend upon its having another property or description (that my action's being the turning on of a light was dependent upon its being a flicking of a switch, for example).

2.2 Sometimes it makes perfectly good sense to speak, as Danto once wanted to speak in every case, of one action's depending upon some other different action. In order to put them on one side for the time being, I shall indicate what sorts of example make such talk appropriate.

In the example of my summoning up an image of a friend, and that's causing me to write him a letter, one action may be said to depend causally upon some other, definitely distinct action. A different kind of dependence, where the relation between the two actions need no longer be a causal one, is found where something is done to prepare for doing something else. I whip the egg whites so that I shall be able to cook meringues, or I take out my keys in order that I can unlock the door. A third kind of case is provided by actions composed of parts that are actions in their turn. If I make a cake, there is a series of things I do – weighing flour and beating the mixture among them – and I would not make the cake without doing them. Or if someone ever dances the waltz, then he puts his left foot forward, his right foot sideways, ...

Perhaps three species of basicness are illustrated in these examples – causal, preparatory, compositional, we might call them –, so that someone's summoning up an image may be *causally* more basic than his writing a letter, his getting the key out *preparatorily* more basic than his unlocking the door, his moving the left foot *compositionally* more basic than his doing the waltz (cp. Baier, 1971 and Danto, 1973, for broadly similar notions). But if these three are species of basicness, then their genus is not the same as that of the species which originally concerned Danto.

Danto recognized that one could not say of every action that it depended for its existence upon some other action; and he looked upon the task of characterizing basic actions as that of ensuring that there be some actions (or of ensuring that one's theory of action should not entail that there are none). He was right to say that certain actions would not exist unless there were others that caused them, made way for them or composed them. But then we had better establish the existence of the actions that cause, prepare for or compose others. If only the basicness of something will legitimate an action as an action, we need to establish that every action, whether or not it is more basic causally or preparatorily or compositionally than some other, has its own basic description or property.

2.3 Saying that *descriptions* (or *properties*) are the more or less basic things might suggest that there are some action-kinds, collected together in virtue of satisfying a single description, all instances of which are basic, and that there are other action-kinds all instances of which are non-basic. But in fact it will normally be insufficient to know of a certain description that it is satisfied by an action, to tell whether or not it is a basic description of that action. Some actions of a single kind and described as of that kind may be basically described, others not. I might simply raise my right arm, for instance; and then 'raising my right arm' will (on many views) be a basic description of my action. But I may also raise my right arm by using my left arm to operate a pulley that raises my right arm resting in a sling; and there 'raising my right arm' specifies the action using a description of it that nobody would call basic to it. If there is any substance to the concept of basicness, we may expect that for any particular action there is a basic description of it, but we should not expect that there are descriptions which basically describe all the actions that they can be used to describe.

In order to keep straight on this, we shall shortly talk of pairs ⟨*a*, *d*⟩ where *a* is an action and *d* a description of it. (I note that there is no confusion in speaking of *the things that are done* when there is an action as more or less basic. Things done correspond to kinds of action, and descriptions of actions determine kinds of actions. I hope that it can be left an open question whether the philosopher's English in which we speak informally about basic action commits us to an ontology of kinds, of properties, of descriptions . . . .)

3

3.1 With these preliminaries concluded, we are in a position to see what lay behind Danto's account, and to show that there is an acceptable concept of basicness that resembles Danto's in using *causation* essentially.

We need first the idea of an *action description's introducing an effect-descrtiption* (where an *action* description is one *possibly* true of actions). Thus 'a turning on of a light' introduces 'a light's going on', 'a flicking the switch down' introduces 'the switch's going down', 'a breaking$_T$ of a glass' introduces 'a glass's breaking$_I$'. In each case the applicability of the action description to some event entails that there is some other event to which the introduced description applies. There may be cases where it is hard to decide what effect-description if any is introduced, or where the introduced effect-description will sound rather contrived. But the idea of an action-description's introducing an effect-description is no worse off than an intuitive idea that I have constantly traded on – that of describing an action in terms of what type of effect it actually had (and cp. Appendix B § 1 and n. 5).

I shall say sometimes that *a pair* ⟨*a, d*⟩ *introduces an effect.* If we have a particular action *a*, and a particular description *d* true of *a*, then the effect-description introduced by *d* will denote some particular effect among the effects of *a*, and the effect it denotes is introduced by ⟨*a, d*⟩. To take an example: the description 'the library's blowing up$_I$' is introduced by 'the blowing up$_T$ of the library'; but the particular blowing up$_T$ of the library by Bill who planted a time-bomb at noon introduces a particular effect when thus described, namely the library's blowing up$_I$ at 1 p.m. (There is a point of detail here: a single ⟨action, description⟩ pair may introduce more than one effect. Suppose someone throws a book across the room and in doing so knocks over and breaks several glasses in succession. Then 'breaking a glass' introduces 'a glass's breaking$_I$' which denotes several different events even relative to the single action in question. Because nothing turns on such cases, however, and because they could easily be accommodated with a little complication, I shall continue to speak of *the* effect introduced by a particular ⟨action, description⟩ pair.)

Applying this terminology, then, and avoiding Danto's talk about causally related actions, we have a universally applicable definition of *causally more basic*, basic$_C$.

A description d of a particular action a is a more basic$_C$ description than another description d' if the effect that is introduced by $\langle d, a\rangle$ causes the effect that is introduced by $\langle d', a\rangle$.

Thus descriptions of turnings on of lights as *flickings of switches* will ordinarily be more basic$_C$ than their descriptions as *turnings on of lights*, because, in the ordinary way, the switch's going down causes the light's going on.

A slightly more complicated kind of example is one in which there are branches in the causal chain leading away from someone's action. Suppose Sykes is driving along and suddenly brakes$_T$ the car. The car's braking$_I$ causes it to swerve, and as a result of its swerving (i) a pedestrian cries out, and (ii) there is a collision. Then 'Sykes's braking' is more basic$_C$ than 'his making the car swerve', and that in its turn is more basic$_C$ than either 'his making a pedestrian cry out' or 'his causing a collision'. But if there is no causal relation between the pedestrian crying out and the collision, then neither of 'his making the pedestrian cry out' and 'his causing a collision' is more basic$_C$ than the other. This shows that 'more basic than$_C$' does not obtain between some pairs of descriptions of a single action; but that is only because the relation 'more basic$_C$ than' replicates up to a point the properties of the causal relation itself, and not all pairs of events that are effects of some single event are related to one another by 'cause'. (Sometimes descriptions may also tie for basicness$_C$, because different descriptions of a single action may introduce the very same effect.)

For a third illustration of how 'more basic than' behaves, consider 'indirect' arm raisings$_T$. If someone on a particular occasion uses his left arm to lift his right, then 'his moving his left arm' is a more basic$_C$ description of what he did than 'his raising his right arm'. This is so, because the former description introduces 'his left arm's moving', the latter 'his right arm's going up', and in the circumstances his left arm's moving caused his right arm's rising.

Note now that even where a man raises his right arm quite directly, there is going to be a more basic$_C$ description of his action than 'raising his arm' – to wit 'contracting his muscles'. This description is more basic$_C$ because what it introduces is causally antecedent to the man's arm's rising$_I$. So we are forced to say that descriptions of actions that take one inside the body are more basic than their bodily movement descriptions. But this seems to be exactly right, if a genuinely causal notion of basicness is at issue.

3.2 So much for *more basic$_C$ than*. But what of *the* basic$_C$ description? Well, we should presumably regard any description that introduces no effect at all as even more basic$_C$ than a description that introduces some effect, because descriptions become more and more basic as the effects introduced are more and more immediate, and the introduction of no effect – the introduction of the null effect, as it were – can be seen as a limiting case of this. So we should think of a description of *a* that introduces no effect as in reality a description that introduces *a* itself. Then the notion of 'more basic$_C$ than' has application even where such a description enters. And taking this line, we can say simply that a description is among *the most basic$_C$ descriptions* – is *one of the basic$_C$ descriptions* – if there is no other description that is more basic$_C$ than it is.

There will always be a basic$_C$ description of an action as 'a trying to . . . ', then, if what I have argued is right. 'Trying to move the arm' does not introduce any effect, because an event can satisfy this description but not cause an arm to move (even if it is generally true that someone's trying to move his arm causes it to move); and it is the same with any description of an action as someone's trying to do something. If some versions of physicalism are true, then there will also be neurophysiological descriptions that tie for the title of the basic description (cp. Chapter Eight, § 2.3). And descriptions even less interesting than neurophysiological ones will count as among the basic$_C$ ones, like 'the event that happened at *P* at *t*'.

4

4.1 *Hand movings* will not be basic in respect of the basicness just defined. This is no criticism of the notion, except in the view of someone with the prejudice that the only interesting sense of 'basic' must be a purely causal one. Even descriptions like 'contracting the muscles' alert us to the fact that *bodily movements* are not the most basic things in any obvious sense of *causally* basic. But we need to ask why Prichard and others should have insisted that we move our hands *directly* or *just like that.* If we could answer this question, perhaps we should understand what lies behind some other, more engaging concept of the basic.

Prichard may seem to have supplied an answer himself. He claimed that if we ask 'How did I move my hand?', this cannot mean 'By causing what did I cause it?', although that is what the question would mean if asked of an action done indirectly (cp. Chapter Four, § 5.1). There is something right in this. We can regard the question 'How did you ϕ?' as an instruction to an agent to redescribe his ϕ-ing, using a new description '—', so that he can truly say 'I ϕ-d by —-ing'; and then, where 'ϕ' is instantiated by 'move the hand', the agent may very well tell us that no new description fills the bill: 'There was nothing *by* doing which I moved my hand.'

We could try to catch this in a definition of a new *basic*, 'basic'*:

> A description d of a particular action a is a more basic* description than another description d' iff '$x\,[d']$ by $[d]$' is true in virtue of a's occurrence.

(In such formulations, '[d]' and '[d′]' represent whatever grammatical transformations or recastings of 'd' and 'd′' are needed to make them appropriate for their slot.) And we appear to have further support for this definition in the fact that the agent who sets out to contract his muscles is liable to tell us 'I contracted my muscles by clenching my fist'. If he speaks truly, the bodily movement remains the more basic* item here.

But this ignores something important. If we press Prichard's question 'How do you do it?' asked of moving the hand, then it surely can be taken in the way that Prichard denies to be possible, and it can even receive an answer of the kind that Prichard ruled out. 'I moved my hand by contracting certain muscles' is a correct and causally explanatory reply, since the agent may have learnt that it is his contracting those muscles (i.e. his causing them to contract) that causes his hand to move. It is true that the agent will not normally give this reply himself. But I think that whoever finds fault with it will discover that he has implausibly to deny that physiologists are concerned with the question *how*, or *by what means*, animals move (cp. *how* food is digested) when they give causal accounts of animal movement, including human movement.

Muscle contractings$_T$ are not the only obstacle to using 'basic*' to capture the intuitive notion of basicness. Until we get back to the point of the causally most basic descriptions of an action, we can construct a 'by' sentence that reflects the causal order wherever we can find one description to be more basic$_C$ than another. And this means that there will be a corresponding true 'by'-sentence for many physiological claims about what goes on inside the body when we act. Ordinarily, of course, the physiologist will speak of events such as impulses in efferent nerves, pulls of muscles on tendons and bones, . . . ; and his claims will not be cast as claims about action. But any sentence that tells of an event that is a more or less immediate effect of an action can always be matched with some sentence about an action. Take any kind of event that the physiologist would mention in telling his story of what happens between brain and body when movements of certain kinds are made. Then we can imagine that the physiologist, using suitable apparatus, could arrange for the agent to see a record of an event of this kind. If what the agent sees is something that he brings about in acting, then his bringing about that event, among others, is his acting. But his mind need not be filled with all the details of his doings for those details to have a place in an account of what he does; and the occasion when the agent first sees that he brings such events about is not the first time that he brings them about. Bringing events like these about was what he was always doing, without knowing it, when he made movements. And now if the agent learns that he brought about two events, the first of which caused the second, then he has learnt something about how he made a movement, that he brought about the second *by* bringing about the first.

Prichard was right to say that 'How did I ϕ?' means 'By causing what did I cause [the event that 'ϕ-ing' introduces]?', but wrong to suppose that this question has no application when we get back to the things that we do directly. Like all of those philosophers who have thought that what is basic is what is not done by doing anything else, Prichard neglected a large class of 'by'-sentences. (Of course it is easy to neglect what we know and care nothing about.)

4.2 The causal account of 'more basic' ('more basic$_C$') coincides at certain points with the account ('more basic*') that uses 'by' essentially. But there are important differences between the two.

In the first place, the 'by' notion imposes a more fine-grained discrimination among degrees of basicness than the causal notion does. Take for example 'He greeted her by waving at her' and 'He contradicted himself by saying that he had been home at 10 o'clock'. On the new 'by' account ('basic*') 'his waving to her' and 'his saying that he had been home at 10' will be less basic descriptions of actions that the sentences report than 'his greeting her' or 'his contradicting himself', whereas on the previous, causal account ('basic$_C$'), there is no distinction between the descriptions on either side of 'by' in respect of basicness. (At least if we think that her being waved to does not *cause* her being greeted. Compare Goldman (1970), and note that we could easily modify and expand the account of 'basic*' to reflect his ideas of *conventional generation, augmentation generation* and *simple generation* in the present framework.)

A second difference between 'more basic$_C$ than' and 'more basic* than' shows up in the case of a man who learns at golf that he must follow through with his club if he is to improve the accuracy of his shots. After practising his drives, he hits the ball correctly *by* following through. There is no question of the relation 'cause' obtaining between the event introduced by 'his following through' and the event introduced by 'his hitting the ball correctly': the motion of his club after its impact with the ball hardly causes the ball to be carried in the proper direction and for the proper distance. But it seems also that this use of 'by' is not to be explained merely by noting that we can discriminate more finely between descriptions of actions than their introduced causal relata allow. What we want to say here is that hitting the ball correctly is the golfer's *end*, and that following through is his *means* to that end.[1]

[1] The golfer may seem to supply an appealing parallel for anyone who takes Thalberg's view of why it is that we say 'He contracted his muscles by clenching his fist'. (I am indebted to Mr J. M. H. Shorter who drew my attention to the case in order to make this point.) What the golfer does by following through is hit the ball correctly; and his hitting the ball correctly is apparently thought of either as a part of his following through or as a part of something of which his following through is also a part. What we are apt to say the physiologist's subject does by clenching his fist is contract his muscles; so why not suppose that the cases are analogous, and agree with Thalberg that his contracting his muscles is a part of his clenching his fist? Well, there is one obvious difference between the cases that will remain even if we do take this view of the relations between the events in the muscle contracting case. Whereas the event that is the golfer's continuing his stroke after his club hits the ball is an action (dependent for its existence on the larger action it partially composes), the event of the fist's clenching$_I$, which is supposed by Thalberg to be the part of the action of fist clenching left over when the action of muscle contraction is subtracted from it, is *not* an action. (Remember it is not the action of clenching$_T$ the fist, since, unlike that event, it is caused by the muscles' contracting$_I$.) That is, even if we did think that muscle contracting$_T$ and fist clenching$_T$ were related as part to whole, and that the existence of a part of the right sort depended upon the existence of a whole of the right sort, we still should not say that the difference between the part and the whole is the agent's doing anything. But in the golfer's case, it appears to be the fact that there is something more for him to *do* than simply hit the ball with his club which makes the 'by'-sentence right.

In my view the crucial difference between the two examples is that we do not have 'He followed through by hitting the ball correctly', whereas we do have 'He

Such examples might encourage the thought that 'by' itself is sometimes a purposive notion. If it were, then we could still understand well enough why 'by' coincides as far as it does with the causal notion we defined, because what a man has it as his purpose to achieve by doing something rests upon what he thinks his doing that thing will cause to occur in its turn. It may then be tempting to claim that there are two senses of 'by'. Only a purely causal sense will account for the physiologist's claims about movements, it will be said, and we must recognize also what we might call a teleological sense, because that alone will enable us to give an account of what it is to do something directly. But the fact that 'by' yields something more fine-grained than 'more basic_C than' does not help in arguing for the existence of a separate teleological 'by', since 'by' retains its fine-grained character in sentences that do not deal with things that were intentionally done. And the fact that 'How did he move his hand?' can be taken in two ways does not assist the case either. It is a quite pervasive feature of questions that ask for explanations that the sorts of response envisaged by the questioner are very different according to his concerns. We must remember, too, that 'basic_C' was not contrived to reflect a prior notion given in any English word. To respond to the discovery that the 'by' notion is not fully registered in the notion of 'basic_C' by saying that the causally basic corresponds to one 'by', but that there is another, overlapping 'by' which accounts for all the remaining cases and which will help us to define a new notion of *basic*, seems, in the absence of any principled means of spelling out the difference between them, an arbitrary and lazy stipulation.

In fact the problem of giving a systematic account of a univocal 'by' is part of a much more general problem. Many causal or quasi-causal words, such as 'effect', 'result', 'because', 'since', 'as', 'in virtue of', can figure in a true sentence even where no causal relation obtains between two events and partially accounts for the truth of the sentence. 'He said that *p* with the effect that he contradicted himself.' 'He hit the ball correctly because he followed through.' Words like 'effect' and 'because' make attributions of connections between states of affairs or conditions which can be, but need not be, grounded in causal

---

clenched his fist by contracting his muscles'. And for me it is this last sentence that counts. I remain agnostic, here as in Chapter Two, whether or not it is actually true that we contract our muscles by clenching our fists; cp. Chapter Seven, § 2.2.

connections between events. (Cp. Kim, 1974; but, taking a different view of individuation from me, he states the matter quite differently.) It seems that a notion of *dependence*, such as that used in § 2.1 (and in Lewis, 1973), might elucidate all of the words from a certain class which includes 'by' (though there is more to be said about 'by' as its distinctive syntax reveals). And if there are causal dependencies wherever there is causation, then that would explain why causal connections should be one species of connection that these notions can so consistently be used to record. I think, then, that to develop an account of 'by' would be part of a much larger project using resources and treating notions beyond any that we shall need here.

VI

BASIC ACTION AND TELEOLOGY

1

There must be some truth in the thought that what is basic is what is not done by means of doing anything else. But there is no notion of 'by' that supplies on its own the idea of means that is needed here. What we require is not the broad idea of how things are done, but an idea of what the agent conceives of as his means; it is the agent's response to Prichard's *How*?-question on which we need to focus, not the physiologist's response. But we can take the agent's point of view by attending to what he did intentionally, I think. Thus[1] :

> A description *d* of an action *a* of agent *x* is more BASIC than another description *d′* of *a* iff in virtue of *a*'s occurrence '*x* intentionally [*d′*] by [d]' is true.

[1] A different suggestion is that the BASIC description is the most basic* (or basic_C) description under which the action is intentional (cp. Hopkins, 1978). But this has the consequence that where a man intends to contract his muscles, *muscle contracting* is the BASIC thing, although it is not what he thinks of himself as doing directly. The present definition, where the scope of 'intentionally' extends to the end of the 'by'-phrase, has the result that moving the body remains basic in such a case. (But Christopher Peacocke has shown me that the definition still mismanages certain cases. Suppose *x* takes a drug in order to block one of two alternative neural pathways, and then moves his hand with the intention of moving it by exciting motor units along the other pathway. Then, as it stands, the definition wrongly takes excitation of these motor units as BASIC. We need a qualifying clause to exclude (roughly) those things intentionally done by *x* whose being thus done is owed to the existence of an action preparatorily more basic than *a*. (Nothing that follows is altered by this.))

> A description of an action is the BASIC description of it iff there is not other description MORE BASIC than it.

I claim that this encodes what has been meant in a great deal of the talk of basicness. But the definition is to be tested by examining its consequences.

It is not uncontroversial what the consequences should be, however, because there is no consensus about what the basic descriptions are. The chief disagreement arises over the claim (made by Danto, and accepted with reservations by Goldman) that bodily movements are always the basic items. Counter-examples to this that are offered include such things as *speaking sentences, tying shoe laces, typing the letter 'p'*. These are all things we can do quite directly, it is said – and rightly, it seems to me. (See Baier, 1971; Annas, 1978.) More evident counter-examples are provided by cases where an agent gains such control over the internal workings of his body that bringing about changes inside himself becomes something that he can do at will. Some philosophers refuse to allow that there are actions at all in such examples, but I suspect that they do so precisely because their accounts fail to admit that anything except a bodily movement could be basic.

I shall start with an account of 'intentionally' (§ 2.1). By putting it to work in particular cases (§ 2.2), I shall show that the definition does confer some special status on bodily movements, but also treats correctly the controversial examples where, despite the dictates of others' theories, bodily movements are intuitively not the basic things (§ 3). A new and more interesting formulation of the central notion will emerge *en route* (§ 2.3).

2

2.1 A certain natural model of action explanation links what is done intentionally with the cognitive and affective states of the agent (cp. Davidson, 1963, 1976). The general idea is that a person in acting shows himself as seeing something as something that he favours (wants, thinks good, or whatever); and he believes that a way of bringing about what he favours would be for him to G, that for him to F would be for him to G, that for him to D would be for him to F, and so on, until finally there is something he can do directly, and his doing that *via* the series of means, D, F, G . . . , will, he believes, enable him to have what he wants. Now if he F-s because he believes that by F-ing he will G, then in the standard case, he intentionally G-s by F-ing. This step, connecting beliefs with intentional features of actions, is what matters here. It means that if we can pick out someone's action using some description *d*, then, if we can credit the agent both with an attitude that reveals that he favours some state of affairs, and with a set of beliefs about means to ends which connect our description *d* with the description that shows this action as favourable for this agent with this attitude, then we may have found something he *intentionally* did; and if we have, then we possess a rudimentary explanation of his action as we had described it. We can understand why he did that.

We should notice that the means-end relations cited as contents of beliefs need not always correspond to relations between the results of something that we pick out as a single action. Sometimes they correspond in this way; when a person moves his hand through a certain path, for example, we consider that movement as a whole, and we say that he made it because he believed that he would thereby light a match. But sometimes when we say that a person ϕ-ed because it was a means to ψ-ing, the relation between his ϕ-ing and his ψ-ing is not identity but the relation that obtains between actions when one prepares for or partially constitutes another: for example, when a person moves his hand and thereby lights a match because he believes this is something he must do in order to light his cigarette; or, more trivially, where we explain why his hand moved through a part of a path by saying that the movement was part of his moving his hand through a larger path, and by connecting the movement through the larger path with the agent's views about what he was achieving. This shows that we can explain an action without saying that the agent found anything desirable about it in itself. And it shows that the kinds of basicness we shall be concerned with now will include the preparatory and compositional kinds that were illustrated in the last chapter.[2]

[2] (a) The model would need refining to accommodate unsuccessful actions, and to distinguish between flukes and straightforward successes; and it would need extending and qualifying to provide any sort of analysis of *means-end*.
(b) Given the connection between 'try' and 'intentionally', we should now predict that someone's trying to ϕ may be his doing something that is preparatory to his ϕ-ing, or something that is potentially a part of his ϕ-ing. I was able to ignore this in Chapter Three, where my arguments exploited another sort of example.
(c) When discussing the identities of actions, I said nothing about counting them. The fact that we need not have a method of counting actions to be in a position to explain them reinforces me in my belief that nothing needs to be said here. Cp. also my (1979).

Notice also that our explanations do not tell us what thought processes, if any, the agent engaged in before acting. It is not said that an agent who intentionally G-s by F-ing must have thought to himself beforehand 'If I F now then I will G', so I desire to F'; it is only said that he must believe that to F would be to G. Again, for him to G by F-ing intentionally it is not necessary for him to have formed the intention to F or to G. Perhaps it is not even necessary to have intended to F – let alone to have formed the intention to F – to have F-d intentionally (cp. Wright, 1974). And so the most unreflective and habitual actions can be accommodated in the style of explanation envisaged (and we can resist the suggestion (e.g. of Hopkins, 1978) that we may always credit agents with a series of complex and causally related *desires* to do one thing by doing some other).

The ordering of descriptions as progressively more BASIC reflects the beliefs about means and ends that the agent manifests in performing any action. At some point we reach the limit in a series of descriptions under which the action can be explained using the model. For at some point we run out of means-end beliefs which we can attribute to an agent in order to account for his doing what he did. Then we reach *the* BASIC description, which says what wasn't intentionally done by doing anything else.

2.2 If someone utters the sentence 'Grass is green', then, even though his mouth makes certain movements – his tongue touches his hard palate with his lips parted and then touches his teeth as his lips close slightly . . . – , he does not make these movements with his mouth because he believes that they are a means of saying that grass is green. For most probably he does not have any interesting beliefs about how he moves his mouth when he says that or says anything else. But if he has no beliefs about moving his mouth in a particular complicated way, then it is wrong to say that he intentionally moves his mouth in just that complicated way, or that by moving his mouth intentionally in that way he intentionally utters the sentence. (Not that these are things he does *un*intentionally.) So his making movements of the mouth of this sort is not what is BASIC.[3]

[3] Of course we could always specify how his mouth moved by reference to what he said, and then we should have a bodily movement description of his speech act which tells of something he intentionally did. But this could support only a trivialized version of the thesis that a bodily movement description is basic, because we cannot usually make out any difference between what someone

What makes the example of a speech act a striking one is the fact that the beliefs at issue are usually not even present. But the real question to be asked is whether particular beliefs should be cited in explaining performances. A belief cannot be cited if it is not present, of course, but it may not need to be cited even if it is. Most (orthodox) typists need only a moment's reflection to tell us that they type the letter 'p' by moving the little finger of their right hand very slightly to the left and upwards by one row of the keyboard, and by pressing the key they find there. And perhaps their readiness of response if asked how they type will convince us that this is something they already had a belief about when asked. But we can still wonder whether it is *because* they have beliefs of this sort that they make the movements they do when they type. It might be rather that they make these movements only because they are the movements that need to be made to type and they know how to type and want to type. (Compare explaining someone's (non-intended) muscle contractions by saying that in fact those muscles had to be contracted if he was to clench his fist and that he knew how to clench his fist and wanted to clench his fist.)

Again some people can trill certain phrases of piano music to a certain standard with their right hand, but not with their left. The difference is presumably not to be accounted for by a contrast between presence and absence of knowledge of how it is done with the right hand and with the left. That is not enough to establish that there is no interesting bodily movement description that could figure in any rational explanation of an exercise of the skill, since it is still possible that the man who trills with his right hand believes that he has to make movements of his fingers in some specific, complicated serial arrangement, and still possible that we should see such movements as movements that he makes because he believes that this is the way to trill the phrase. But even if it were correct to credit him with beliefs of the

---

believes it is for him to utter the sentence *s* and what he believes it is for him to move his mouth in such a way as to utter the sentence *s*.

Some people hold that we must have interesting beliefs about our mouths and vocal apparatus if we are to be able to speak at all. But they block the possibility of our making *discoveries* about the mechanisms of speech: what is it to learn exactly how one's mouth moved, unless it is to acquire a belief about this? (Anyone inclined to say that we have 'unconscious belief' or 'tacit knowledge' about what goes on inside us when we act will not find anything significant in BASICNESS. But I shall not argue against his assumptions, because the arguments against them can and should be given independently.)

complexity required for there to be interesting candidates for a basic bodily movement description, there might continue to be a reason to think that the beliefs do not explain the performance. If we thought that the triller, though he knows in detail how he trills, might just as well have forgotten, then we should have such a reason. Even if he had forgotten, it would not make any difference to his being able to trill like that now. And sometimes we do think that theoretical knowledge, even if it was needed to come to be able to do something, may not be needed to continue in possession of that ability.

Another reason for discounting particular pieces of theoretical knowledge for purposes of the explanation of certain performances is that practice is essential to the development of some skills. By practising one may acquire a capacity. One may at the same time learn more about how something is done; and that may be incidental, or it may be a step to the acquisition of the capacity. But if the practice was necessary, then whatever was learnt in practising may be expected to figure somehow in an account of performances. We say, for instance, 'Now he can do it, because now he has mastered the motor routine.' And if this is the truth about him, then there was a new skill that he had to acquire and his beliefs about its exercise give at most a partial explanation of his doing what he does.

In other cases it is clearer that no substantive theoretical knowledge has to be learnt in the process of acquiring a skill. When we teach children to tie their shoe laces or to ride bicycles, what we hope to communicate is a practical capacity, and to do so by encouraging imitation and approving movements of the right sort. It seems wrong to say that anything much in the way of theoretical knowledge about how these things are done is imparted.

2.3 The inadequacy of the 'by'-locution on its own to capture the idea of basic action led to the introduction of 'intentionally' into a definition. And the connection between *intention* and *belief* that is revealed in the scheme of explaining actions then made us ask what beliefs an agent manifests in particular performances. But we have come now to talk about different kinds of *knowledge* that are needed in the exercise of skills. In part that reflects a shift of interest – a shift from a concern with the different degrees of basicness of actions of all kinds of kinds, to a concern with *the* basic descriptions of all of the actions of particular kinds that agents can reliably undertake with success. The move puts us in line with a question that has interested philosophers in talking about basic action: they have wanted to know what sorts of things a person may have the standing capacity to do 'just like that'. And this brings us to talk about knowledge. If someone can reliably ϕ successfully, then typically he has knowledge, not only beliefs, about the means of ϕ-ing. So we arrive at the idea that, in order to do something that is BASIC for him, an agent need have no theoretical knowledge to the effect that an action of one kind will be an action of another kind. His theoretical knowledge can come into account only when what he does is something that is NON-BASIC for him.

This leads to a new way of looking at what it is for something to be BASIC, which, with only the loss of some of the detail, summarizes the old:

> The kinds of action in an agent's repertoire that are BASIC for him are those which he knows how to do, and knows how to do otherwise than on the basis of knowing how they are done by him.

The crucial distinction here is between knowing *how* and knowing *how to*, and it would be blurred if we followed Ryle (1949, pp. 28ff.) in marking the distinction between practical and theoretical knowledge with a contrast between knowing how and knowing that. For to know *how* something is done is to possess theoretical knowledge that it is done in a certain way. So we need at least to call the practical kind of knowing knowing how *to*.[4]

It will not always be easy to say what knowledge we need to attribute to agents in making explicit and complete our explanations of what they do. In giving explanations in practice, we can usually leave much of their knowledge out of account, because it is common knowledge about the obvious. But even where the knowledge is taken for granted, it has a place in a full account, at least if the supposition that the agent lacked the knowledge would make some aspect of his performance impossible, or harder, to understand. It may sometimes be genuinely indeterminate how much knowledge would be explanatory –

[4] Even this may be problematic. Someone who has never driven a motor car may say that he knows how to drive none the less, and say that on the basis of his possession of theoretical knowledge how it is done. Again, someone who has become paralysed may say that he knows how to drive on the basis of having once been able to. But as Ryle used 'know how' – i.e. 'Know (at t) how to' –, he took it to be incompatible with 'not be able (at t) to'. This is what I too intend. Perhaps I should really say 'knows how to do and is able to do'.

as some of our examples suggested. But then perhaps it is rather indeterminate what the basic description is. At any rate, this need not tell against the several claims (3.1-3.4) of the account to have explanatory power.

3

3.1 We can understand why it should be tempting to think that moving the body is always the basic thing, even if that is not quite accurate.

A full theoretical story of how someone does something will include many specialized truths as well as some familiar truths that every agent knows. Such a story starts inside the body, and it applies descriptions to an action that are progressively less causally basic (and, owing to the finer discriminations among events that specialists may make, the descriptions will vary with respect to compositional basicness). At some point, it will go through a description that is teleologically basic (BASIC). When the story is past what is BASIC, some of the descriptions it applies will be of real concern to the agent himself. But it may be possible to look back before the point of the BASIC description and remain in touch with his interests. Someone who wished to improve his elocution, for example, might want to know how speech sounds are produced, even though it would ordinarily be no handicap to speech to know next to nothing about this. So we can distinguish the stage at which the descriptions might conceivably be of use to an agent, and the stage at which the descriptions include those that an agent needs to know to do the thing in question. Even before the first stage, there may be a great deal more that can be said, but it could not be of help to an agent who wanted to know how he could do something himself (except in the special case of wanting something to happen inside oneself; see below). One can exploit knowledge that that switch's going down causes that light's going on in order to turn on the right light. But to be told which neurons' firings are causally connected with the emission of a certain sound is of no earthly use to anyone concerned to make that sound himself.

Up until some point, then, the story is not in touch with the agent at all. That is where it talks of things that are outside his control. The point when it first connects with his interests may be earlier than the point of the BASIC, and it is usually the point where the story begins to speak of the minimal bodily movements. This shows that the body marks one significant limit, albeit a vague limit.

3.2 We can still say what it should seem right to think that people who come to be able to control events inside their bodies, like the firing of specific motor units or the rate of heart beat, increase their repertoire of basic action types. (See e.g. Basmajian's experiment, *Science 141* (1961), cited by Nagel (1969), and the vast literature on biofeedback.)

Some people learn to do these things anew. But just as most of us cannot say how we move our bodies, so these people have no idea how they effect the internal changes; *a fortiori* they do not act on the basis of knowing how it is that they do so, and what they do is BASIC for them.

We should need a better understanding of the notion of control to provide an explanation of why it is that the voluntary bringing about of changes is ordinarily limited to the bringing about of changes in a world that starts at the surface of our bodies, or an explanation of how it is that we can sometimes expand the range of what is voluntary. Presumably for an organism to have control, it must be in a position to make changes that are contingent on changes it can detect. (Perception is the handmaid of action.) And we cannot control the workings of our bodies for the most part, because for the most part we aren't sensitive in the right way to what goes on inside us. Sometimes such sensitivity can be achieved through effecting correlations between internal and external change – as in biofeedback; sometimes, perhaps, it can be achieved through new capacities for introspection or through heightened self-awareness. But if we properly understood why the regulation of some kinds of states of affairs is typically under voluntary control, and why the regulation of other kinds of states of affairs is typically not – why the mind sometimes takes care of the body and why the body sometimes takes care of itself –, then perhaps we should be closer to knowing how consciousness has evolved.

3.3 Where a physiologist teaches a subject to make particular sorts of events occur inside him intentionally, by teaching him what happens when he moves his body, the repertoire of basic actions is not expanded. For here the belief that moving one's body in a certain way brings about such events *is* used in bringing them about. If he wants, the person can now do something (such as contract muscle *m*) because he wants to do *that*. He did it before he had the physiological knowledge, but no explanation of his doing it then could mention his wanting to do it.

Unless we allowed the descriptions of actions to start before the point that is ordinarily BASIC, we could not accommodate these cases at all. Moreover we could not make the right sort of contrast between them and the previous cases where we think that new abilities are acquired. For practical purposes, the theoretical knowledge that enables us to bring such things as our muscle contractions within the scope of our intentions is of little avail. It is the causal future and not the causal past of his bodily movements$_I$ that will concern the man who wants to further his ends. But still, the theorist ignores the causal past of our bodily movements$_I$ at the expense of making it quite mysterious how a man could ever obey a physiologist's instruction to make certain sorts of change take place. The matter need really be no more perplexing than it is perplexing how we can do anything else that we want to: we make use of our knowledge of causal relations between things that we can do directly and other kinds of events.

3.4 The account also enables us to see why it should be wrong, despite the prominence I have given to *trying*, to allow that trying to act is always teleologically basic.

To give complete agent-oriented explanations of actions, we have to think of a person as having knowledge about something in his basic repertoire. And it is presumably through experience that a person comes to have knowledge of what he can do. But we do not find out in experience what we can try to do, except as we have learnt from experience some of the things that we can actually do. (It may be a necessary condition of ϕ-ing intentionally that one tries to ϕ; it is not a necessary condition of knowing how to ϕ that one knows how to try to ϕ.) For no one can set out to try to do anything unless he is in a position to conceive of himself as having certain abilities (cp. Grice 1971). That shows that some beliefs that a person has about what he can try to do can never replace beliefs about what is basic in explanations of actions. We do not say that a man is able to raise his arm because he believes that his trying to raise it results in his raising it, and 'trying to raise it' is not then a teleologically more basic description than 'raising it'. This point explains how it is that the regress of trying (at the end of Chapter Four) is usually halted at the very first step. And it reflects the fact that *trying to ϕ* is not, in the terms of genetic epistemology at least, more primitive than *ϕ-ing intentionally*. (Compare Wittgenstein's claim that *its looking red* cannot be taught before *its being red. Zettel*, § §417-25. And see Chapter Nine on action and perception.)

4

The case for basic actions has commonly been made on the grounds that we shall be led to a regress without them. It is generally put by saying 'Not every action can be performed by performing other actions' or 'Not every action can be dependent upon another'. But in addition to the other difficulties that I made for these formulations, I think that two quite separate claims are run together. There are two different kinds of regress that must be avoided.

I prefer to say:

(i) 'In a series of descriptions of an action that speak of the action in terms of its effects, we should be led to a regress unless we could say that at some point the action may be characterized in terms of its most immediate effect, or of no effect at all.' I argued that actions can, as *tryings*, be described in terms of no effects at all. This emerges in the fact that *tryings* are causally basic ($basic_C$). And the claim that actions occur inside the body is merely the claim that the causally basic descriptions of actions need allude only to internal events.

(ii) 'Among the things a person knows how to do, some of them he must know how to do "just like that", on pain of needing to ascribe to him indefinitely many distinct pieces of knowledge to account for his ability.' This poses a very different threat of regress. It shows that there must be teleologically basic (BASIC) descriptions. It also shows why, in the practical and epistemic situation that is our common lot, we should not concern outselves with those descriptions of actions which make it manifest that actions are inside the body. The significance of agency for persons as agents and interpreters of agents begins with the teleologically basic.

VII

ACTION AND CAUSATION

1

Up to this point I have made uncritical use of event causality in explicating agency. It has now to be shown that event causality is prior to agency in respect of explanation, and that an account of human action does not require some other notion of causality. In this chapter I oppose theories which hold that some concept from the sphere of action is at least as fundamental as any concept of causation that has application in the world beyond the agent.

The view that *agency* or *agent causation* is indispensable to any complete account of causal processes colours an enormous number of different doctrines, and has had a long philosophical history. But in justifying my own account I can concentrate on two particular theses that will stand hostage for the general viewpoint. The first is the manipulability or actionist theory of causation held by von Wright, according to which agency is conceptually prior to causation (§ 2). The second is the theory of agent causation, defended by Chisholm. This says that the causal character of the connection between a person and what he brings about has to be characterized using a primitive causal relation whose first term is a person, and not an event (§ 3). One may think of the first theory as primarily about *causation* – that it has to be understood in terms of agency –, and the second as primarily about *agency* – that it cannot be completely understood in terms of event causation. It would be easy to think that by making as free as I have with event-causality I have excluded both of these theories and all others like them.

What is true is that in founding everything in event causation, I have refused to entertain a certain ancient doctrine. The primitive notion of *cause*, we are told, was derived from the relation between a man and his action (see J. L. Austin, 1956, p. 202 in 1970; Collingwood, 1940, p. 324 ff.). And certainly in ancient and medieval times, causation in the absence of human action was typically construed either as divine action, or as the action of a material object invested with a power, an object whose nature it was to realize certain ends. Even at a time when science had come to use the notion of event causation, Reid objected to it as unintelligible. He thought that the idea of cause and effect in nature must be arrived at by analogy, from the relation between an active power and its products; and he held that any other model of causation was quite obscure. Like most of his predecessors, then, Reid believed that the subjects of the causal relation must always be things in the category of Substance, whether mental or material substances.

I have disregarded this long-standing doctrine. But the two theses I am to consider might be thought of as modern, toned-down versions of Reid's doctrine. As far as I know, the two theses are not held jointly by anyone today. But if they were put together, then they would yield a position with much of the force of the ancient one that Reid in modern times espoused. If someone accepted both Chisholm's and von Wright's theses, then he would believe that there is a special relation of causation peculiarly operative when people do things, and another causal relation which serves to link events outside agents but is still to be understood by reference to the notion of action. Human agency would be given a very special status in our conceptual scheme.

2

2.1 It is a characteristic thesis of von Wright and others who hold the manipulability theory that an account of causation must appeal to the idea of human agents' producing one thing by producing another. (See von Wright, 1971, 1973, 1974; for a more modest account, Gasking, 1955; and for an account restricted to certain brands of causality, Collingwood, 1940, Chs 29-32.) Thus von Wright offers this definition of causal asymmetry:

> In the cases where I bring about *p* by doing *q*, *q* is the cause and not *p* (1971, p. 75).

Von Wright's use of 'do *q*', especially when it is co-ordinate with 'bring about *p*', seems to import a confusion between actions and their effects. Indeed there appears to be no way to give the definition a consistent reading if expressions denoting the same sorts of thing are inserted at the places of '*p*' and '*q*' within it. And it would introduce a circularity to say that an action is counted as a *doing* of something if it is described in terms of an effect that is *causally prior* to any that we allude to in calling it a *bringing about* of something. But perhaps the definition can be reformulated in such a way as to escape this difficulty, and accord with what von Wright meant. Using terminology from Chapter Five, I propose:

> If *e* and *f* are effects introduced by descriptions of an action of mine as a P-ing and as a Q-ing (respectively), then *f* is the cause and not *e*, if I P by Q-ing.[1]

But if this reformulation is faithful to von Wright's intentions, then, given his own beliefs about the example of the man who intentionally contracts certain muscles, we find a contradiction. It will be true, so far as von Wright is concerned, that the man contracted his

[1] Two features of the reformulation might lead someone to query it.
(a) It makes use of the idea of 'introducing an effect', and that idea was defined in terms of event causation, so that the reformulated definition may seem to help itself to the notion that it is meant to explain. This feature may not matter to von Wright, however, whose principal purpose is to understand the direction of causation. To know what effects are introduced (as we must to apply the reformulated version) is not yet to know the causal ordering among those effects (which may be all that von Wright's definition is supposed to inform us of).
(b) The '*p*' and '*q*' of von Wright's definition are said to range over generic events, whereas my '*e*' and '*f*' range over particulars. However, *p* and *q* are said to be generic events *in particular cases*; and this is got across in the reformulation: 'P-ing' ('Q-ing') corresponds to a type of event, and *e* (*f*) is an event that occurs if there is a particular P-ing (Q-ing).

Von Wright recognizes that if the project is to reveal actual causal asymmetries, it cannot be enough to give a definition that speaks only of generic events. The definition must concern not merely such sentences as 'F-ing causes G-ing' (which is compatible with 'G-ing causes F-ing' – alarm bells' ringings cause movements of persons *and* movements of persons cause alarm bells' ringings, for example); it must also deal with sentences like 'This F-ing causes that G-ing' (which may be presumed incompatible with 'That G-ing caused this F-ing'). The point suggests the indispensability of talk of particulars. We could ask von Wright whether he means to subscribe to an ontology of cases, and to tell us what cases are. I suspect that 'a case' of a generic event is actually a particular event, and that, however implicitly, any formulation of the thesis of the asymmetry of causation will speak of particulars.

muscles by moving his arm, but it is also true (according to the arguments of Chapter Five) that he moved his arm by contracting his muscles. Applying the definition, we are told that contracting muscles is the cause and not the arm movement, *and* that the arm movement is the cause and not the muscle contraction.

One might use 'more basic than' instead of 'by' in the definition, in an attempt to avoid the inconsistency. Von Wright himself did this:

> One can distinguish between cause and effect by means of the notion of action . . . [To distinguish them where they are simultaneous] requires that there is some basic action, i.e. an action which we do directly (1971, p. 76).

The notions of 'more basic than' defined in the last chapters certainly have the needed property of asymmetry. But even so, neither of them is suitable for defining causal priority. If the causal notion of basic were used, then the analysis would be circular, because, in order to know what is causally more basic, one must know how the events that result from some action are related to one another by 'cause'. If the teleological notion were used, then the province of causation would be definitionally restricted to the range of things that are intentionally brought about. Yet there are surely many events that are caused, but not intentionally caused by any human agent. (It is a standing objection that the manipulationists make the scope of causation unduly narrow, cp. Mackie, 1974, pp. 170–1. But the problem is considerably aggravated when the definition mentions explicitly what is *intentionally* done; and we have seen that the notion of intention is needed to distinguish between the *causally* and the *teleologically basic.*)

Perhaps it will be thought that von Wright for his part need find no difficulty in all this. We saw in Chapter Two that he is prepared to allow that there is backwards causation if a man intentionally brings about an event inside his body. So von Wright will deny that the physiologist's 'by'-sentences are true, and say that there are no causal connections between the events inside us when we act except where we intend to bring such events about. In that case causal direction and 'basic' may both be defined in terms of 'by' without the definitions producing any contradictions (cp. 1971, p. 68). But something else we saw in Chapter Two shows how hard it is to take this point of view seriously. It is more surprising to be told that there is only backwards causation when a man intends to contract his muscles (or bring about some internal event or other) than it is to be told that there is backwards causation whenever a man acts. And it is something yet more surprising that von Wright has accepted, if he defines causation in terms of (his understanding of) 'by', and swallows the consequences. He has to hold that it is solely in virtue of an agent's being able to say on occasion 'I meant to contract those muscles, I did so by moving my arm' that causality holds at all between muscle contractions and arm movements, and that when there do suddenly start to be causal relations between such events, they run backwards – from the body's moving to the contraction of the muscles.

2.2 Of course a contradiction will threaten anyone who believes that 'by' behaves in asymmetrical fashion, if he also accepts that both of the following things can be true of a person on a single occasion:[2]

(1) He contracts his muscles by clenching his fist,
(2) He clenches his fist by contracting his muscles.

Von Wright's account of causation might be regarded as one way of dealing with the problem created by our disposition to accept the belief about 'by' in addition to (1) and (2).

One reaction to the problem is to deny that there is any difficulty in accepting both (1) and (2) on a single occasion, e.g. on the grounds that 'by' expresses a notion of dependence between states of affairs, and that there is no inconsistency in thinking that an action's having one property depends upon its having another and that its having that other depends upon its having the one. *By* could then be thought of as the expression of a notion more fundamental than causation, on which the causal relation between events is derivative. As we learn to control and manipulate our surroundings (it could be said) we learn of means and ends and of relations of dependence between things we do, and our conception of such dependences, being contained, for instance, in many of our action verbs, precedes our coming to recognize that some of the dependences are founded in causal connections.

[2] I intend by ' "By" behaves in asymmetrical fashion' not the claim that 'by' is an asymmetrical relation between individuals (it isn't: cp. Chapter One, § 2.4), nor the claim that 'He ϕ-d by ψ-ing' and 'He ψ-d by ϕ-ing' are everywhere incompatible (they aren't: cp. Chapter Five, § 2.2). The claim is rather that there cannot be an action a, two descriptions d and d' of a, and effects e and f introduced by $\langle a,d \rangle$ and $\langle a,a' \rangle$ respectively, such that 'He [d] by [d']' and 'He [d'] by [d]' are both true in virtue of the occurrence of a, e and f. (I ignore again the 'point of detail' mentioned and set aside at p. 70.)

This is an attractive picture of the relation between 'by' and 'cause'. It enables us to say that it is a *sine qua non* of a person's possessing the concept of 'cause' that he should know what it is to act in the world, even if we wish to stop short of agreeing with von Wright that *agency* comes first in the order of analysis or definition. And it leaves open the question whether 'by' behaves asymmetrically.

In order to settle that question, which would be to determine whether (1) and (2) can be simply reconciled, we should need a very much more detailed account. I myself suspect that a theoretically sound account of 'by' will commit us to rejecting one of sentences (1) and (2), and I am disposed to deny that (1) is ever true. I show my hand here, because I have endeavoured until now not to commit myself on this. But none of my arguments has depended upon accepting the literal truth of (1), or the asymmetrical behaviour of 'by'. The reader may decide about these things for himself.[3]

This leaves a third reaction, which is von Wright's. He denies that (2) is ever true. And, more astonishingly, he denies the scientists' claims about the causation of human movement that I take to underlie (2). Apparently he thinks that we cannot study man as a part of nature, because man's experiments have to be seen as interventions in a world to which the idea of causation only gains application through accounts of those interventions. I should say, on the contrary, that we cannot study man as agent, unless we are prepared to see his actions as the beginnning of causal chains whose descriptions can be given independently of any account of his intentions.

2.3 To understand what it is for states of affairs to be brought in line

[3] In an attempt to soften the claim that (1) is always false, I note two points: (a) Arguments in Chapter Two purported to show that if ever (1) be true, then it is true whenever a man clenches his fist, whatever his intentions. (The same goes for (2): if we accept (2) because we think that muscles' contractions cause fist's clenchings, then we are unlikely to believe that (2) can be undermined one day because a man then sets out to contract his muscles.) Thus it would be wrong to suppose that in assessing (1) and (2) we can confine attention to someone who *intentionally* contracts his muscles.
(b) My account is custom built to explain why we should hold to (1) where we do. If someone has an intention to do something causally more basic than what is teleologically basic, then he knows what events cause events that he can produce directly. An agent's knowledge is typically of a different sort: we know what events are caused by events that we can produce directly. But perhaps we ignore the difference, and conform our descriptions always to the typical case.

with someone's intentions, we require a conception of those states as depending upon his actions, and of his actions as depending upon his intentions to produce those states. If we are to think of his intentions as directed onto states in the world, then we have to think of his actions as issuing in results that match the content of his intentions by way of the actions making the right sort of difference to how the world is. In explaining someone's non-basic actions, we have, I claimed, to cite his theoretical knowledge of what follows on what when the body has moved. I now suggest that in order to see ourselves as having knowledge of the right kind, we must take our concept of causation to have application independently of what we bring about. Certainly the knowledge that a person needs to be at liberty to do the things that he can't directly do is knowledge that can be acquired through experience of his own interventions. But we could not think that there was any such knowledge to acquire, unless we were able to consider causal processes apart from our manipulations. Even if I can do something by moving my body in a certain way and I want to do that thing, still, until I know that I can do that thing by moving my body like that, I have no reason to move my body like that. But to have a reason I must have causal knowledge that can serve as a basis for my intentions. To do things intentionally I must be able to think of nature as something constant and continually at my service.

If we accept that so much is needed to make sense of agency itself, then we must be prepared to admit that there are discoverable causal processes that subserve action but that do not figure in an account of agents' intentions; and then we shall reject von Wright's idea that no events that an agent makes happen can be causally prior to the point where his intentions take off. (I suspect we all resist such causally prior events when we say 'I contracted my muscles by clenching my fist'. It is as if we thought that nothing could depend upon our actions unless it depended upon what, in acting, we conceive of as dependent on our wills.)

Some people think that if the view of causation required to make sense of action has the effect of absorbing our actions into nature, our conception of nature as the servant of our actions must be displaced by a conception of ourselves as at the service of nature. Then our wills are the subjects of the same inevitabilities as we take ourselves to exploit in realizing our wills, and we find ourselves at the beginning of a path that leads to the conclusion that none of our actions is free. If we are convinced that we are free, then we shall probably want to reject the idea that there is any such path. But more drastic measures can be taken to defend our freedom. Von Wright brings *action* itself into the descriptions of the causal processes.[4] And Chisholm insists that descriptions of processes of nature are inadequate to account for the things that happen when a person acts.

3

3.1 Chisholm thinks that nothing is a free action if it is not caused, and that nothing is a free action if there is some event that is a sufficient causal condition for it. And because he takes it to be incontrovertible that human beings sometimes act freely, he is then led to seek a novel account of the causation of actions. The proposal is that in cases of action, causation relates *persons* to events. Consequently actions are caused, but determinism, which concerns causation by events, is supposed not to touch the belief that actions are free. (See e.g., 1969.)

Chisholm has sometimes described his doctrine as the doctrine that *agent causation* is irreducible to event causation (e.g. in 1976b, p. 199). This might mean that if we take a sentence which, in speaking of an agent's causing something, speaks of an action, then we cannot paraphrase it correctly using simply the word 'cause' as 'cause' relates events (along with the name of the agent and the description of the event he produced that figured in the original sentence). But if that were all that the irreducibility of agent causation came down to, then it would surely be true. What would be dubious is whether it has ever been denied. No event is the action of a person unless something about that person's states of mind occurs essentially in an explanation of that event; and so we cannot get it across that there was an *action* without somehow including something which entails that that sort of explanation is in the offing. (Chisholm assumes that 'Agent *a* caused *e*' entails that there was an action, and *pro hac vice*, I shall reluctantly concur. Cp. Appendix A, § 3.)

Clearly there is more at issue than this weak irreducibility thesis.

[4] In (1973) and (1974) von Wright sometimes denies that his thesis is one about conceptual priorities. I have discussed the conceptual thesis, because it is that which I have to defend my own against, and because I think that if the primacy of agency over cause is to be used as the cardinal premise in an argument that freedom is compatible with universal event causation, then more than epistemological primacy will be required (cp. Mackie, 1976).

Granted that 'Event *e* caused ——' cannot simply supplant 'Agent *a* caused ——', it remains a question exactly which causal notions will have to be kept in the paraphrases of sentences that say what a person caused. Chisholm will answer that, whatever else we include, we shall never make do using event-causality solely. (See also Taylor, 1966.) But how could this answer solve the problem of freedom? If the determinist's thesis is not to offer any threat to free action of the sort that Chisholm envisages it offering, then it apparently needs to be denied that actions are caused by events. Yet Chisholm's claim that we cannot avoid talking about causing by agents if we want to talk about actions need not prevent us from thinking that, concerning every event, including the events that are actually actions, there is some true statement saying that it was caused by an event.

In his earlier writings, Chisholm said that, where there is agency, 'at least one event is caused, *not* by other events, . . . but by the agent' (1966, p. 17, my italics). This conception will suit anyone who thinks of himself as literally interrupting the course of events when he acts (butting in, as Prichard used to put it). But Chisholm has come to reject that idea. He now believes that there are events that cause the events that agents cause, but that these events, unlike other events, are not sufficient conditions for their effects (1976a, p. 69). Since this belief is not entailed by the ineliminability of agent causation, Chisholm's doctrine of agent causation can scarcely guarantee our freedom. However, my concern is with the doctrine itself, not its motivation, and I shall pursue the problem of freedom no further.

3.2 Chisholm says that it is not in question that human beings cause events. I agree: we talk about persons causing many different kinds of thing, and often what we say is true. But then we also talk about stones and flames and cricket bats causing things. So if our ordinary talk lent support to the ineliminability of agent causation, it might lead us much more generally to think, with Reid, of causation by substances as primary.

Chisholm's definitions of agency reveal why he takes causation by persons to be a special case. Agents *causally contribute* to events, and they may contribute *indirectly* or *directly*. If an agent causally contributes to an event indirectly, then he causally contributes to an endeavour, which, in the standard manner of event causation, contributes in turn to that event. But to his endeavours themselves, the agent contributes directly. And it is the direct causal contributions that are made only by persons, according to Chisholm, and these that cannot be understood in terms of event causation. (See e.g. 1976a and 1976b. I have condensed considerably.)

Where I think that the occurrence of a trying is not enough for an action, Chisholm similarly thinks that an agent's causally contributing to an endeavour is not enough. We are agreed that there has to be some further event of an appropriate kind, caused in the ordinary way, and that this further event is not itself the action. So Chisholm and I both think that actions are not bodily movements$_I$, but, in some sense or other, the causings of bodily movements$_I$ (and the assumptions of Chapter One are not in dispute). The difference between us is that I say (roughly) that it is in virtue of an event's being an endeavour of an agent that the agent can be said to cause what it causes, whereas Chisholm believes that it is necessary to look beyond the endeavour. We have to posit the agent's causally contributing to the endeavour (directly) in order to explain how the agent can be said to have caused (indirectly) what his endeavours cause. But if Chisholm retains his claim that every event is caused by another event, then it seems that the agent's causally contributing to his endeavour must be an event that causes his endeavour. And it then looks as if Chisholm has simply inserted an event before the endeavour into his account of action, in order to have something that is ineliminably an agent's causing something.[5] For our ordinary understanding of agency contains no presumption in favour of the existence of such events. Endeavours are precisely not the sort of things that we can say that agents cause: compare 'He caused the disturbance' with 'He caused his endeavour (/trying/attempt) to disturb'.

The response may be that we have to see agents as causes of their actions or endeavours, that otherwise we shall be obliged to see actions as events that are caused by events and cause events like any others, and that then we shall have lost the idea that persons are held responsible for what they bring about. But everyone accepts that not any old event is an action, and nobody supposes that we succeed in characterizing actions just by thinking of them as having causes and effects. To say

[5] For a demonstration that the agent's causally contributing satisfies Chisholm's own criterion of eventhood, see Donagan (1977). (Donagan also shows that, in spite of Chisholm's assumption that events are generic, it would actually remove certain difficulties in Chisholm's account if we were allowed to modify it and treat events as particulars. For this reason I leave on one side the disagreement between Chisholm and me about ontology.)

that an event is a person's trying to do something is already to give it a very special status in his life. (Compatibly with this, and less contentiously, it can be said that no event is an action unless the agent's thoughts and wants cause that event to occur.)

3.3 If we do not ordinarily say that agents cause their actions or endeavours, and if this is not something that we need to say in order to distinguish actions from other events, then the agent-causationists surely have a duty to provide us with some reason for thinking it is true. Collingwood is the only philosopher I know of ever to have produced any argument here.

Collingwood starts with the point that when a man is afforded a motive for action by some influence from outside, then that influence may be said to cause him to act (1940, p. 293). But then, if a man's motives are independent of others –

> if he does for himself, unaided, the double work of envisaging the situation and forming the intention, which in the alternative case another man (who is therefore said to cause his action) has done for him, *he can now be said to cause his own action* (p. 294).

As Collingwood states the case, there is a shift between the initial statement of the premise and the premise as it is actually used in deriving the conclusion. The initial claim (used in all of Collingwood's examples, p. 290) is that some things, including other people, may cause *x to act*: after the shift he has it that a person may cause *x's action*. But a general claim about causing ourselves to act seems to be more obviously vulnerable to criticism than a general claim about causing our own actions. This should make us distrust the agent causationists' talk about causing actions. We seldom use it in describing particular cases in everyday life, and we may be blind to what is wrong with using it generally. When we turn to a statement that gets its life outside the formulation of philosophical theses (and which may or may not be literally equivalent to the agent causationist's claim) – 'We always cause ourselves to act' – we feel that we know better how to assess it.

Sometimes we do cause ourselves to act, and we do then cause our actions. But I have suggested that this is so only in certain special cases (cp. Chapter Five, § 2.1 and § 2.2). If someone leaves his keys inside the house, then he may cause himself to pick the lock later. What Collingwood's idea of affording motives suggests is a slightly different type of case. If a man has the difficult task of breaking a piece of news to a friend, but cannot trust himself to do so spontaneously, then he may decide to do something that will create circumstances in which he will scarcely have the option not to break the news; and perhaps in this way he may 'afford himself motives', and cause himself to do the difficult thing. But in examples like this, where we make for ourselves opportunities to do what doesn't come easily (or make for ourselves obstacles against doing what comes too easily), there is once again a prior *action* that causes the future action. I say that for a person to cause an event is for an action of his to cause it, from which it follows that our own actions may be among the events that we cause, but that they are so only if our own actions are among the events that our own actions cause.

Still, Collingwood thinks that a man *x* causes his own action whenever he envisages the situation and forms an intention unaided, because *x* then does exactly what *y* does when *y* causes *x* to act. The parallels he hopes to exploit are less than perfect, though. *x* can envisage the situation for himself: *y* cannot literally envisage it for him. *y* can inform *x* of the situation: *x* cannot literally inform himself of it. (To inform one must know the situation; to be informed one must fail to know it.) Again, *y* cannot form *x*'s intention to act: *x* does form that intention. In persuading *x, y* acts with the intention that *x* should form an intention to act: *x* in forming his intention to act is not usually doing anything with the intention that *x* should form an intention to act.

Some lack of analogy is to be expected here. Only I can stand to my mental life in that relation, whatever it is, that makes it mine. But what obstructs the parallels is more than this truism – it is some of the actual features that make a man's life his own. Someone's having thoughts and wants and capacities can suffice for his own action, but they cannot suffice for anyone else's. We do not usually have to work on our minds in order to bring it about that we do things, but we have to work on the mind of another if we are to bring it about that he acts. We use influence on others, but we can act ourselves without causing ourselves to act.

3.4 Can we not, in spite of the differences between others and ourselves, assimilate the events that occur in a man's mind to the events that go on outside him when he is caused to act by someone else? If an agent's thoughts and wants cause an event to occur, might it not just as well be said that he, the agent, CAUSES it to occur?

There can be no objection to saying this, provided it is recognized that the new 'CAUSE' is not the 'cause' that we ordinarily use with names of persons as subject. To say that an agent caused *e* is (*modulo* Chisholm's assumption) to say that some event that was his action caused *e*. But then if the sentence '*A* CAUSED his action' means that *A* caused his action, it says that an action of his caused an action of his.

We should ask the agent causationist how an agent is related to an event that is his CAUSING his action. If the agent does not CAUSE such an event, then the event will prove to be simply something that causes the action; and so long as event causality is thought to stand in the way of genuine agency, no such something can assist in providing what is essential to action. But if the agent does CAUSE his CAUSING his action, must he then not also CAUSE his CAUSING of his CAUSING it . . . ?[6]

The regress here is of the sort that Gilbert Ryle's argument exposed. One must not postulate as a necessary condition of the occurrence of an action the occurrence of a separate event that is also an action. That shows that if 'CAUSE' is to be used to give a mark of action, it cannot be taken in a sense in which an agent's CAUSING something is the same as his intentionally doing anything. And then one wonders what sense it might be supposed to have.

Well, there is one perfectly good thing that an agent's CAUSING his action could be. Suppose we take CAUSE to be the relation between a man and his action, and let '*a* CAUSE *x*', be coextensive with '*x* is an action of *a*'. Then we will always cause our actions, and all of Chisholm's claims about causing endeavours will be true. The only outstanding question then is whether or not this relation – *is an action of* – can be adequately elucidated in terms of event-causality.

I have not committed myself on this question. But even if it is established that 'action' cannot be fully analysed in terms of psychological notions and event-causality (see Chapter Nine, § 4.2), that will do nothing to show the propriety of agent causation as a constituent in an analysis, because we do not have any understanding of *agent causation* except as we understand *action*. I believe, though, that we are afforded some understanding of *action* by our conception of causation as a link between events in which agents participate and those events in the world beyond them for which they may be held responsible.

[6] To apply this to Chisholm, substitute 'causally contribute' for 'cause' and 'endeavour' for 'action'. And note that when Chisholm says that his definitions do not entail that we endeavour to endeavour, he is defending himself against the sort of regress Prichard feared, not the sort that threatens Locke. (See Chapter Four, § 4.1 and § 5.3.)

VIII

KNOWLEDGE OF ACTION

1

Some people think that a philosophical account of a subject matter cannot be correct unless it is compatible with our knowing exactly what we always take ourselves to know about the subject matter. I doubt that the maxim can be accepted in full generality. But an account of something can be none the worse for meeting this demand. And I am prepared to argue that my account of action meets it. (If the reader does not mind whether it does, he is invited to skip to the last chapter.) My account has no surprising consequences so far as knowledge of other people's actions is concerned (§ 2). And when it comes to what we know of our own actions, again there are no unwelcome results (§ 3).

2

2.1 One objection to my view is likely to run 'If actions are inside the body, then we cannot see them. But nearly all of our knowledge of others we take to be derived from observing what they do. So your view encourages a specious scepticism about other people.'

The first question that needs to be asked is whether, as this objector presumes, we ordinarily do take ourselves to see actions. What we commonly say is 'I saw him do it', not 'I saw his doing it'. That is, we say that we see people acting – see people who are acting and that they are – and not that we see their actions. Obviously I don't doubt that we see people.

Still, the objector thinks that we see actions themselves, and I am inclined to agree. But he says 'If actions are inside the body, then we cannot see them.' Some doubt is cast on his conditional when we remember that to say that actions take place inside the body is not to deny that they take place in larger portions of space: there is no one place that is *the* place where an event occurs (Chapter One, § 4.1). Perhaps then we see actions in virtue of seeing *some* place where they occur when they occur; perhaps we see actions in virtue simply of seeing the people whose actions they are at the time of their happening. Or again, perhaps we see actions in seeing their effects.

That I say these things does not signify some special difficulty for my position. Anyone who holds that actions start inside the body, for instance, and who thinks that overt bodily movements$_I$ are merely parts of actions, will need to say that we see actions in virtue of seeing parts of them. So he too will have to concede to the objector that actions are not events that take place in their entirety 'strictly before our very eyes'.

Trouble can be made for me here only by someone who has certain rather definite views about what it takes to see something, and who has an account of action on which the perception of actions is left as somehow unproblematic by his own views about seeing. Such a philosopher may suggest that there exists some strict, direct sense of 'see' (e.g. we 'directly see' something only if there is a straight line to our eyes through a transparent medium from each of the points that circumscribe the smallest portion of space that the thing occupies), that even in this strict sense we do see actions, and that it is a fault in any account if it does not allow for that. But his point is good only if the required sense of 'see' can be recognized for the extraordinary sense it is, and it still seem counterintuitive to say that we cannot 'see' actions. Presumably when the required 'see' is applied to the perception of substances, we shall find that we cannot 'see' a table if it is covered by a cloth. I doubt whether there is such a sense, and suspect that any other force the objection enjoys will derive immediately from the belief that actions are bodily movements$_I$.

We can hardly help ourselves to the belief that actions are movements$_I$ when assaying a contrary thesis about what actions are. What we may do, though, is to ask how much we know of the actions of others, without prejudice to any particular theory of actions. And then, provided that we are not too hasty to offer some putatively general account of what it takes to know something through observation, it may prove that my own theory leaves the matter exactly where it was.

2.2 'Surely a thesis about the location of actions will make some difference to what we take ourselves to know', someone might say, 'because it affects a more general question about people's minds. If actions are internal, then they must be mental events. But then, on your account, we observe mental events, and it becomes impossible to explain how anyone should ever have found any attraction at all towards scepticism about other minds.'

Originally it was said that the view of action led to scepticism; and now it is said that it leaves no room at all for the sceptic to make his case. But it is a curious idea that locating actions inside the body could somehow convert them into mental things. (The *point* of the distinction between the mental and the physical is unlikely to turn on questions of location.) Equally it would be strange if, by arguing that some of the things we know about go on inside people, one found a new way to prove that we have access to their mental lives – as if we could claim insight into the mind of others only if we could get a better sight of the insides of their bodies. But neither the sceptic nor I think that.

If we want to learn about people's states of mind, then we can rely on our ordinary observations of people interacting with the world, if we can rely upon anything. For something can be seen as the doing of something that is intentionally done – as an action – only as it can be taken to reveal the mental states of its subject. And it can support the ascription of mental states to him, only if it can be seen as satisfying some description that can be used in stating the content of his states (cp. the model of action explanation at Chapter Six, §2.1). But then making sense of a man cannot be a matter of observing what goes on beneath his skin: this is a portion of the world that he does not normally conceive of himself as affecting. The point can best be put in terms of an earlier distinction: a description of an action that is causally more basic than the most teleologically basic description is of no use to someone who sets out upon discovering what a man thinks and wants.

2.3 Even if we need not know any causally basic, 'internal' properties of actions to know about actions, and to be in a position to defend certain philosophical claims about them, still someone might think that my own claims are bound to have consequences for what it *would be* to know about actions seen close up and picked out in, say, neurophysiological terms. If we imagine ourselves having sight of a chain of physiologically articulated, causally related events which culminates in a bodily movement that occurred because and only because someone did something, then exactly where in the chain should we say that we find the action? Supposing that we can know that all the events before a certain point are definitely earlier than the action, then do we have a method for picking out from among the things occurring after that point that event or sum of events that is the action?

These are questions about how the neurophysiological descriptions of what happens when we move relate to our ordinary ways of talking about actions. But nothing I have said suggests any *a priori* reason why there should be a tight fit between the two vocabularies. Our only route to the extension of the predicate 'action' is by way of our understanding of action descriptions; and if the neurophysiologist develops his classification of events independently of the interests we have in saying what we do, then there can be no presumption that what he singles out is the same as what we single out using our everyday vocabulary. It is not merely that reductionism is false, and that we should not expect to find any simple neurophysiological predicate with the same extension as any action predicate. Even in the particular case, why should we expect that when we refer to some action what we refer to is something caught by the neurophysiologist's classification?

Any attempt to locate actions by way of neurophysiologically specified events must rest upon asking what truths can be stated by introducing the neurophysiologist's words into the locutions that we use for saying what we do. I have held that actions are earlier than muscle contractions, because I take that to follow from what we say when we apply to the contractions of muscles our understanding of what it is to bring things about. I also suggested that there are causal relations between things which are the effects of actions and which occur before the muscles contract. But again that was because I think that we accept 'by'-sentences that link descriptions of internal events, and think that a proper understanding of 'by'-sentences will take 'by' as linking descriptons of actions in terms of effects. Someone who doubts that 'by'-sentences are in place here may hold that our concepts of action, which had their life before anything was known about neurophysiology (and which can apparently be used by people who believe that some spiritual force sets our bodies in motion), do not provide us with anything to say in the language of action when we are presented with the internal events close up. According to this view, the neurophysiologist's discoveries will at most enable us to say something about what actions themselves consist in. But I believe that our responses to discoveries show that as we know more and more about what goes on inside us, we increase our scope for describing actions as actions. That is, the neurophysiologist can provide more and more detail about the events we cause to happen, about the immediate effects of our actions.

What is certain is that there is some limit to the importation of neurophysiological vocabulary into a description that picks something out as an action. Otherwise we lose actions altogether. There may be a temptation to say of every one of the events in our imagined sequence leading up to his movement$_I$ that the agent brought it about, so that, however far back we go, we can find something to say about his action seen as a cause of the event we encounter there. The temptation to speak like this is explicable. Since we aren't in a fit state to do anything with our brains wide open to view, it is in the nature of the case that someone has always to see effects of an action (for instance records of it on a screen wired up to the brain) if he is to see the action. And it is in the nature of the concept of action that we only ever see things as actions when we see them as having some effect or other. But if anyone ignores either of these points, he may pick something out using words that actually constitute a causally basic description, but continue to speak as if he were picking out something in the way that we normally pick out actions – in terms of effects. The pressure to keep on seeing actions *as* actions (as causes of other things) then prevents him from seeing anything as the event that is, simply, the action, now not looked upon as the cause of anything else. But if actions are the events that cause what we bring about in acting, then there is a point in the neurophysiological sequence at which there occurs the cause of whatever it is that had the effects by means of which we may describe something as an action. At that point we no longer find events that the agent made happen, because at that point we find the action, his making happen of so many things. Perhaps the brain marks the limit, and all of the relevant things that happen there make up the action. Or perhaps our concept of action is not invested with such determinacy that we can draw any sharp line (at this level of resolution) between his causing things and the things he caused.

Anyone who takes my denial that actions are bodily movements$_I$ to land me with some new obligation to say what actions 'really' are will find it unsatisfactory that I give an answer to the question *Which is the action*? that leaves so very little settled. But I believe that all the common ways of talking about actions, which have the virtue of being recognizably ways of talking about actions, must be enough to show us enough of their reality.

3

3.1 So much for what we know of the actions of others, and of what we might come to know of them. I turn now to our own knowledge of our own actions. There is more to be said here, because a person can know what he does otherwise than by means of making observations of himself of the kind that others could make of him.

Professor Anscombe has suggested that people make a mistake as a result of recognizing that they have a special source of knowledge of their own actions. She thinks that people have erroneously been led from there into postulating items such as willings that are meant to serve as the objects of the agent's peculiar knowledge – as if our consciousness of what we do were some extra, to be added onto the events that everyone else has access to. I have to show that my claims about trying are not to be seen as the product of some comparable mistake.

Anscombe calls our own special knowledge of our own actions knowledge without observation.[1] She thinks we go wrong when we see that there are two sorts of knowledge of our own actions. This

[1] Anscombe herself takes it that an agent's special knowledge is something he has *in addition* to the observational knowledge that others have. But it might be thought that it is rather that an agent's own knowledge *supplants* knowledge of the kind that others have. O'Shaughnessy, for example, claims (1963) that we can never observe our own actions. I doubt that the claim can be accepted in full generality. But I think one can see why the idea of observation should sometimes seem problematic applied to one's own actions. At least in the case of complex activities, where one has to concentrate in order to succeed, it is necessary to adopt a practical attitude towards what one is doing which may preclude the adoption of that theoretical attitude from which observation typically takes place. This may show that *observational knowledge* is not a happy term to describe what agents can know about their actions by seeing and hearing events in the world. But I shall adhere to Anscombe's terminology none the less. The contrast she intends is clear enough, even if it is unclear exactly how it should be made out.

leads us to suppose that there must be two objects of knowledge, she says, and then we suppose that there must be something like a willing that we can know about without observation, and a different thing, which results from the willing and which observation tells us about (1957, pp. 51-2). Willings then get introduced to play the part that they play in Locke's and Prichard's accounts, the things that only introspection can discover.

Now obviously there is no quick argument such as Anscombe imagines. But it seems to me that there is a perfectly good route from the existence of two kinds of knowledge to the existence of two pieces of knowledge. It proceeds by demonstrating that what we know without observation can be different from what observation tells us of.

Suppose that someone sets out to turn on the light in the hall, and, because he does not know which switch is which, he turns off the light in the kitchen. He knows what he has done through seeing the result. But that does not make him think he is mistaken about what he set out to do. He knows that he meant to turn on one light, and tried to do that, but actually turned off another. Since discovery of results does not here affect what he takes himself to know without observation, it seems that we might (in principle) always describe someone as having knowledge of what he tries to do, even where there is in fact a perfect match between that and what he actually does. Thus we may say in general that there is something – what he tries to do – which observation does not usually uncover for him, and something else – what happens thereby – to which his observation is often relevant. These two things are surely distinct things that may be known, so that the two sorts of knowledge correspond to two pieces of knowledge. (Cp. Donnellan, 1963.) This is not yet to say that the two propositional pieces of knowledge correspond in their turn to two separate items (or events). But at this point we find ourselves in as good a place as any to start on arguments designed to show exactly that. I concluded such arguments at the end of Chapter Three.

Landry's patient, discussed in Chapter Three, might equally have prompted the distinction between the agent's knowledge of trying and his knowledge of what results. There we have someone who does not know whether his arm has gone up, when he does know that he has tried to raise it. So even when the making of simple movements is all that is in question, we may still distinguish two things known. The example reveals that our division between two pieces of knowledge need not rely upon there being two kinds of knowledge in Anscombe's sense. For the knowledge that one's arm is rising got in proprioception is itself knowledge without observation, which means that, when it comes to simple movements, we do not have to trade on a contrast between knowledge with and knowledge without observation in order to argue that different things are known by the agent. (Of course we could always distinguish here between two different species of *non*-observational knowledge – practical knowledge which Landry's patient has, and the proprioceptive knowledge which he is exceptional in lacking. There would then be two different kinds of knowledge to go with the two different sorts of object. But our question is not the question how exactly we should classify kinds of knowledge, but whether there is any division between different kinds that can properly lead us to speak of different objects.)

3.2 Perhaps someone will say that to distinguish between two different things that an agent knows is to present an unrealistic picture of how it normally is with us when we do things. For it is absurd to think that we have two separate impressions of what goes on, one from inside ourselves and one from without, and that in putting these together we arrive at a conclusion about what we have done; and it is obviously wrong to say that a thought about what he is trying to do crosses the agent's mind whenever he does anything. However, it is equally a mistake to suppose that this is the picture that emerges from the claims about knowledge and trying. Why suppose that a possible complexity in our account of a person's states of mind must always be reflected in a complexity in what he is conscious of?

From the fact that someone can be said to know that he has tried to ϕ, and to know of a result of his trying, we cannot conclude that he knows of his action by inference. Indeed I argue from the fact that he knows that he did something to the conclusion that he may also know that he tried to do that, all on the assumption that if he had not been successful he would still have known at least that he tried. So it can be we, not he, who make an inference, and the inference is then the other way about.

It becomes plain that knowledge of one's own action need not be inferential, if one thinks again of Landry's sensationless and blindfolded patient. Imagine now that he knows that he has the capacity to raise his arm, and has no reason whatever to think that anyone will prevent him from doing so. Then when he does raise his arm on some occasion, he surely knows that he is raising his arm. Since he has no way of telling that his arm is going up (except for his knowing that he is raising it), his knowing that he is raising it clearly cannot be inferred from a separate piece of evidence that it rises. Indeed the only thing that could count for him as 'evidence' that he had raised his arm is his certain knowledge that he tried to raise it.

In this last case, we can use the fact of the agent's non-observational knowledge to support the idea that his trying is an event separate from anything that observation tells him of. But there is still no cause to think of tryings as Anscombe thought that others thought of willings, as items that we can learn to recognize as such in ourselves. Provided we hold onto the belief that actions are tryings, we shall see that even our peculiar knowledge of what we try to do may be something we learn to acquire only as we learn to speak with others about what we do and what they do, and about what we try to do and what they try to do.

In Chapter Three we envisaged certain features of a spectator's situation that prompted him to say that he knew that some agent had tried to do something, however odd or otiose it would have been for him to have said that, if those features had been absent. And now, when we think of the agent himself, we see that we can construct special features of the case that make it seem right to say that *he* knows that he has tried (e.g. in the light switching example), and that once again the special features are not such as to alter what normally goes on when someone does something. Still I doubt whether it is possible fully to generalize the argument from the agent's knowledge, as we were able to generalize the argument from spectator's knowledge, and my case does not rest at any point upon paying special attention selectively to what the agent himself knows. But if one believes that agents do try to do everything that they intentionally do, then, whether or not one thinks that consideration of the agent's non-observational knowledge can help to ground that belief, one will very likely hold also that agents *know* that they try to do things far more often than we in practice credit them with this knowledge. It is as well to have noticed that there need be nothing strange in that.

IX

ACTION AND PERCEPTION

1

1.1 If I am right about action, and if those who have recently advocated causal theories of perception are right about perception, then there is an obvious analogy between the concepts. To describe an event as a perception (a perceiving of something) is to describe it in terms of its causes: to describe an event as an action is to describe it in terms of its effects. The analogy is particularly striking if one thinks that an action is an event that takes place inside the body and that the bodily movement$_I$ required for there to be an action is not itself a part of that action. We do not think of events of perception as including the things that we perceive. Perhaps, as I have argued, we should equally not think of an action as including the movement whose occurrence is a necessary condition of its having occurred.

The comparison of my account of action with an account of perception will display the argument of the whole essay in its barest essentials. I hope it will also serve a useful purpose in persuasion: it has been necessary to impute a number of confusions to other philosophers' conceptions of action; but if I can show that these correspond one to one with as many potential confusions about perception, and if it is clearer that these are confusions, then this may lend further support to the account of action.

Grice's theory of perception is similar to my own theory of action (§ 2). And the similarity shows up in a wide scheme of structural parallels between various different accounts of action and perception that people have held (§ 3). Grice aimed at an analysis of perception;

but I shall have to explain why the task of providing an analysis of action goes beyond anything that I have attempted here (§ 4).

2

2.1 Wittgenstein asked 'What is left over when I subtract the fact that my arm goes up from the fact that I raise my arm?' In 'The Causal Theory of Perception' (1961), Grice asked, in effect, 'What is left over if I subtract from the fact that I see a material object the fact that the object is present?' His strategy was to start by demonstrating that an ordinary statement saying that someone perceives some material object *m* entails, but is not entailed by, what he called a sense datum statement. And that made feasible a certain style of causal account of perception. The fact which the sense datum statement conveys is part of what remains when the fact that *m* is in front of *x* is subtracted from the whole fact that *x* perceives *m*; and the rest of the remainder (or what combines with the other necessary conditions to give sufficient conditions), Grice thought, will be a causal condition.

If Grice's analysis was not to be circular, then a sense datum statement *s* must not itself entail that anything is perceived. But if the analysis was to be causal, then *s* must plausibly figure in a conjunction with another statement that said what causes the having of the sense datum, where that conjunction does entail that something is perceived. Compare these properties of *s* with the properties of a statement that says *x* tried to ϕ. I have held that such a statement does not entail that *x* ϕ-ed intentionally, but it does seem plausible that a conjunction of such a statement with a further statement about what *x*'s trying resulted in may entail that *x* ϕ-ed intentionally. These properties are the mirror image of those required by *s* (and we have given a partial answer to Wittgenstein's question).

Grice held that to accept a theory with the special features of a causal theory of perception was 'to accept the claim that perceiving a material object involves having or sensing a sense datum' (1961, p. 123). But if my interpretation matches his intentions, then the analogy suggests that it is not impossible that mention of sense data should drop out from the *s*-statements.

'Trying to ϕ' determines a type of event, some but not all of whose instances are actions, and its instances are actions, only if they cause events in some other, related type. Thus a causal account of someone's having ϕ-d intentionally might go something like this:

(i) There is an event of x's trying to ϕ,
(ii) there is an event of the kind that ⌜ϕ-ing⌝ introduces,
(iii) the first event causes the second.

The ontology of events is explicit here; but that does nothing to interfere with conceiving of the task as Grice did. For finding a class of events, some of which are actions, and all of which are putatively actions and can be characterized independently of saying that they are actions, is simply one way to find a necessary but not sufficient condition of there having been an action. But speaking of events, one can employ the notion of *cause*, an extensional relation, to state the causal condition. (It should be said straightaway that (i) - (iii) do not give sufficient conditions for action. They are used here only to illustrate what could found one possible causal theory.)

It seems then that Grice could have prepared the ground for his own causal theory by finding a type of *event* (the putative perceptions) so characterized that events of the type that are caused in a certain way are actual perceptions of objects. Of course one will want an account of the perception of objects in the category of continuant, and not, or not only of the perception of events. But although this shows that a new complexity needs to be introduced into the analysis (e.g. 'x perceives m only if *the presence of m* causes . . . '), it need not make any difference to the gist of things. 'Event' will have to be understood quite broadly. Neither the things that cause us to perceive, nor our perceivings, are momentary happenings. But a broad conception of 'event' has been intended throughout this essay: events are what we talk about when we talk about causes and effects.

Grice sought a class of *statements*, some of which are true in virtue of a material object's being seen, and others of which are true even though no material object is seen. It is easy to be led from this to the idea that there are objects of sight that are not material objects; these will be the items in virtue of which a statement in the class can be true even if nothing material is seen, e.g. sense data, or appearances, or percepts, or visual impressions. But if one takes the task to be primarily that of specifying an appropriate class of *events*, then it becomes easier to say that there is no object of sight when nothing material is perceived. Rather, there are events that are not perceivings of anything, but that share certain properties with events that are perceivings of material objects.

Grice's claim that sense data have to feature in a causal theory of perception is vindicated, then, if 'sense data' is taken to stand for a class of events. This gives an amusing twist to the traditional sense datum theory; the given, the data of perception are nothing other than what happens (at least) when the world impinges on our senses.

2.2 Grice's own arguments were directed at showing that something like 'Its looking to x as if m were before him' can serve as a necessary condition of x's perceiving m. It is interesting to note that his conclusion could have been supported in very much the same way as I defended the conclusion that we try to do what we intentionally do. (Suppose that a neurosurgeon tells y that he intends, by putting a device into x's brain, to cause x to have a series of hallucinations during some experimental period. Just occasionally, he says, the hallucinations will correspond to reality: whenever x is in a certain place where there is an oak tree, x will have an hallucination as of seeing that very oak tree. Now the neurosurgeon's experiment finishes unexpectedly early, and when y meets x, the device has already been removed from x's brain and normal sight has been restored. They meet in the vicinity of the oak tree and y takes some persuading that x really is seeing the tree. But he says that he always knew that it would look to x as if the oak tree were before him. The point once again is that there is something – concerning how it was with the perceiver x: cp. the agent of Chapter Three – which the spectator y never did make any mistake about.)

If one wishes to adapt Grice's formulation to cover kinds of perception other than vision, one might come to speak of 'its seeming to x just as if he were perceiving m' (cp. Strawson, 1974). Let it not be said that if x's perceiving m is his seeming to perceive m, then it is equally his seeming to seem to perceive m . . . . To charge a vicious regress here is very like making the mistake of saying that if someone's ϕ-ing is his trying to then it is equally his trying to try to ϕ; and the mistake of supposing that superficial form guarantees such an inference was exposed at the end of Chapter Four.

Is the condition of its seeming to x just as if he were perceiving m acceptable, then? Intuitively one thinks that finding the right condition is a matter of specifying a class of events that share certain phenomenal properties with actual perceivings; and, seen in that light, the condition seems right. But it is all too easy to hit upon a class that is too narrow when one starts by reflecting upon what it is like to perceive. When we turn our minds on to our perceptual states we may forget that we often perceive things that we do not notice or attend to and that we are in no position to describe (cp. Quinton 1955). There is no comparable difficulty about *trying*. The things we try to do are not only the things that we are actually conscious of doing. The use of 'trying to ϕ' has not been supported by thoughts about how it is with us when we act, but by the connection between 'trying to ϕ' and 'ϕ-ing intentionally'. And once it is recognized how many more things we do intentionally than we consider doing, or do on the basis of having formed a prior intention, it should be evident that, in marking out actions initially in terms of what we try to do, one does not exclude actions of which we are not reflexively aware.

I suspect that a condition for perception suited to the role that Grice hoped that his condition would play is actually much harder to come by than the parallel condition for action. This is probably the reverse of what has usually been thought, even if neither project has usually been conceived of in quite this way. But whatever one believes about the relative difficulties of the two cases, the main thing is that, at an elementary stage, the tasks can be thought of as parallel. And it may not matter if one thinks that one or other is impossibly difficult, and despairs of specifying a correct necessary condition or class of events in either case. One can still ask what is distinctive about the causal history of all those events that are actually perceivings of some sort, or distinctive of the causal future of all events that are actions of some sorts. In that way, one can take an interest in the nature of the concepts of action and perception, even if the project of finding an analysis is over-ambitious.

2.3 As a rough and ready statement of the Gricean necessary condition in the perceptual case, I use '*x* seems to perceive *m*'. For my purposes it does not matter if this is vague, nor does it matter whether it is always true of a person who actually perceives *m*. Provided it can be understood as a condition true for the most part of someone who perceives *m*, its being no accident that the condition is true of him, I shall have all that I need to extend the parallels between action and perception to the knowledge that agents and percipients themselves possess.

I claimed that a person's knowledge that he tried to do something is distinguishable from his knowing that his trying resulted in some appropriate effect. This is very like a distinction between someone's knowing that he seemed to perceive something and his knowing that his seeming to perceive it resulted from some appropriate cause. With both trying or seeming to see, it appears that there is a certain first-person authority, and it appears that each of these things is, for the person concerned, in a certain way immune from doubt. In both cases, we can characterize a person's state of mind as it were from the inside – as a trying to ϕ or a seeming to see m – in a manner the subject of the state very likely knows about best; and we can characterize that same state of mind from the outside – in terms of its output or input relations, as an action or a perception – in a manner the subject of the state is not especially well placed to know about.

What has mostly concerned philosophers is not this analogy, but something connected with a certain failure of analogy between the two cases. Knowledge of the results of actions is something that can be got independently of knowledge of trying – proprioceptively or by observation; but we cannot in the same way get any separate purchase on the causes of perceptions, on whether our seeming to perceive something has the right kinds of cause. All of the evidence that we have in this case (it is said) is once more evidence that we seem to perceive. It then looks as if we should often be in a position to confirm that we have actually done something, but cannot ever be in a position to get independent confirmation that we have actually perceived something. And it is said, for this reason, that we cannot justify passing beyond the belief that we *seem* to perceive. The result is a general scepticism. Can we ever know that, when we seem to perceive, our experiences are caused by things in an external material world?

One response to this sceptical challenge is familiar: we need not think that our beliefs that we perceive things are inferentially derived at all. (Grice offers this response when he imagines someone objecting against his causal theory that it leads to scepticism.) The interesting thing for us here is that the familiar response gathers momentum so soon as one notices the real congruity of the cases of action and perception.

The fact that a man may know with particular certainty that he tries to do something does not support the conclusion that it is only with lesser certainty and by inference that he can know that he actually does something. Indeed it is possible for someone to have no independent knowledge of the results of his action and still to know that he is actually doing something (Chapter Eight, §3.2). If these points were carried across to perception, they would undermine the contention that a percipient only knows by inference that he is perceiving. A man's certain knowledge that he seems to perceive something is all the particular evidence that there needs to be for him to have knowledge that he does perceive it. And that leads to the welcome view that seeming to perceive something is just one part of the total set of circumstances that give a man a right to be sure that there is something present to his sense organs.

My purpose here is not to refute the sceptic, but to reveal how far the analogies may be pressed. And I hope that I may incidentally gain favour for my account of knowledge of action – at least in the eyes of a philosopher who is already prepared to accept that when a person sees something he often knows that he seems to see it. Provided that this philosopher believes that nothing pernicious need follow from that, then perhaps he will accept that there is nothing wrong in saying that when a person does something he often knows that he tries to do that thing.

So far as knowledge of others is concerned, the case of perception may again reinforce what was said about action. The fact that events of perceiving occur inside people does not make us think that we are barred from knowing what others perceive. We understand others by making sense of how they affect the world, and by doing so in the light of what we can surmise about how the world has affected them.

3

3.1 I claim that correct accounts of action and of perception are in important respects enantiomorphically related – are counterparts like a left-hand and right-hand glove. But what about the accounts that I do not accept? I suggest that they too can be seen as counterparts.

Consider first one rather obviously objectionable sense datum version of the causal theory of perception. It holds that someone perceives an object only if he is caused by that object to perceive some sense datum of it. The trouble with this is that it entails that no one ever perceives anything. For according to this theory, it will be a necessary condition of perceiving a sense datum that that sense datum cause one to perceive a sense datum of that sense datum. But then one must perceive the sense datum of the sense datum, ... The regress here is clearly akin to the Rylean one examined in Chapter Four. (Ryle himself employs a regress argument against a certain theory of perception; but it is a slightly different argument against a slightly different view: 1949, p. 207.)

The lesson of Ryle's argument about action was that one should not say *both* that in order to do something a person must perform a conation which causes his action, *and* that conations themselves are actions. If you believe in conations, then either you must say that they are not actions, so that they do not need to be caused by further conations (Locke and Hume); or else you must say that conations are identical with actions, and that there need not be any causal relation obtaining between things of the two kinds (Berkeley and Prichard). Similarly, if you believe in sense data, then either you must say that perceiving a sense datum is not itself perceiving – not at least in the sense of 'perceive' in which material objects are perceived (cp. the claim that 'act' in 'act of will' does not mean act); or else you must say that sense data are identical with, and not the causes of, perceivings of material objects. This latter is precisely the interpretation that I have wanted to put upon Grice.

In both cases we are faced with a regress of objects: an infinite series of conations (with a consequent regress of actions because conations are taken to be actions), or an infinite series of sense data (with a consequent regress of perceptions because sense data are taken to be perceived). If we want to escape from regress, but we accept a dualist theory, then we can insist that exactly one conation or sense datum is required for each action or perception. But in both cases we can escape from both dualism and regress by affirming identities between the items regressively iterated and items of the sort that we are attempting to provide an account of. That is, we can say that conations are actions, that sense data are perceptions.

3.2 It is important not to underestimate how great a departure from the traditional view of sense data is marked when 'sense data' is treated as standing for a class of events. The traditional theorist meant by 'sense data' the intentional objects of perception, and it will not do to suppose that sense data might serve both as events that are perceivings *and* as objects of perception. Russell once tried to have it both ways (1927). But the upshot was another theory of perception quite as absurd as the regressive account.

Russell was inclined to concentrate entirely upon events, at the expense of continuants, as the things perceived. And this made it natural for him to think of percepts (his equivalent of sense data) as events. Anxious not to make the dualist's mistake of thinking that 'seeing is something "mental", totally different in character from the physical processes which precede and accompany it' (1927, p. 147), he identified percepts with the occurrences in the brain that are perceivings. None the less he clung to the central idea of the sense datum view and thought of percepts as things immediately present to us in perception. But if we see percepts, and percepts are perceivings and perceivings are in the brain, then 'all you ever see must count as inside your brain' (ibid., p. 147).

Russell's strange conclusion stems from a failure to follow through the thought that perception can with all propriety be described in terms of the things that cause it. That failure led him to retain percepts as objects of perception, because he thought that things that are causally remote from the brain could not serve as the objects in the last analysis. Causal processes do precede perceptions on his view, but the processes figure only because they are taken to yield the proper objects of sight in the brain. And so we are offered a causal theory of perception in which the causal element in the concept of perception has been extracted from it.[1]

An account of action as extraordinary as Russell's (1927) account of perception would result if someone combined some of my claims with a failure to appreciate that actions are described in terms of their effects. If one did not take it to heart that the descriptions of actions reach out to the things that actions cause, the thought that conations are actions and that conations occur in the brain would point to the conclusion that we only ever bring about things in our brain. This outcome illustrates how disastrous it would be to adopt my own view about what actions are, but to disregard the fact that a causal element is inherent in the concept of action itself.

3.3 We have seen four theories each of action and of perception. In each case there is a regressive theory, a theory of the kind that I should accept, a traditional dualist theory, and a theory like the one that tempted Russell. We are well on our way to a psychopathology of the philosophies of action and perception – or a reasoned taxonomy of all

[1] In later writings Russell retained the physicalist account but did not draw the surprising consequence – save in the particular case of perceiving the brain of another: in many places Russell insists that a perceiver of another's brain actually sees his own brain. I suspect he kept the surprising consequence there because one finds it so hard to acknowledge that an event is someone's perceiving something when it is seen close up. (There is the same difficulty with action, cp. Chapter Eight § 2.3.) It should be said that only in one passage out of three whole chapters on perception in (1927) does one find the extraordinary view. Except for the particular passage, Russell's talk of percepts might be seen as a quite legitimate attempt to specify a class of events of which the appropriately caused members are perceptions. That Russell saw the need to specify such a class is clear in his (1940) where he speaks of *perceptive experiences*.

possible mistakes. But we shall omit some, if we do not study now a discrepancy between the conceptions of action and perception that have been held.

Sense data, when they are posited, are meant to play the role of intentional objects of perception (whether or not they are also conceived as their causal predecessors). Volitions, on the other hand, are usually thought of simply as causes of actions. And thus, in following what has commonly been believed, we make sense data intermediaries between causes of perceptions and perceptions, but we place volitions behind actions.

This difference between traditional theories of perception and action is reflected in the kinds of account of the two concepts that have been accepted. It is easier to come to think that we only ever perceive things in our brains than to come to think that we only ever act upon our brains. And although a dualist theory of action is available that avoids Ryle's regress, a theory of action is easily caught up in some kind of regress (Chapter Four, §4.2 and Chapter Seven §3.4). It is interesting to speculate why there should be these differences. If I am right to suppose that correct theories of perception and of action are isomorphic up to a point, then why is there a tendency to opt for something regressive in the case of action, and the opposite tendency – to opt for consolidation, as it were – in the case of perception?

First, there is nothing in the perception subject matter to provoke any of the linguistic confusions, like the confusion between transitive and equiform intransitive verbs, which have led people to treat actions as if they were the effects of actions and had to be caused by actions.

Second, there is nothing in perception to correspond to what makes for all the misunderstandings that go along with talk of doing things or of performing actions. Failure to construe the phrase 'do something' (or 'perform an action') on the model of specific verbs of action makes it appear that it reports both a doing (or performing) and a separate thing which is done (or is the action). Nothing similar applies to the phrase that we use to talk about perception in general – 'perceiving things'. For whereas the question 'What did you do?' must be answered by saying simply that there was an action of some particular kind (which thus had a certain sort of effect), an answer to the question 'What did you perceive?' will directly mention something separate from the perception. With 'perceiving something', then, it is not a mistake to interpret the words as verb with external accusative, and grammar keeps one clear of one possible regress. (For perception it would be possible to take the external for an internal accusative. To attribute such an error to Russell would help explain how he came to talk of perceiving percepts, and thence to suppose that what we see is in our brains. It is as if, abetted by the cognate relation of 'perceive' and 'percept', Russell treated 'percept' as the internal accusative of 'perceive'. Looked at like that, his attempt to eliminate the subject – by what he thought was the only means of avoiding the dualist's act/object distinction – resulted in the elimination of the object.)

Here we are taken from a grammatical diagnosis of the difference in what has been thought about action and perception to a third point, which is a deeper difference. When we reflect upon our own actions and perceptions, we are apt to think of conscious occurrences having some immediate content. It is surely this that ushers in volitions and sense data. (Cp. Hume's 'I mean by the will . . . nothing but the internal impressions we feel and are conscious of when we knowingly give rise to any new motion of our body'.) If we accept this, and go on to ask how we are related to the contents of our experience in each case, we are likely to give different answers. We stand back on our actions and look on them as our own product, but in perception we conceive of ourselves as more intimately connected with our sense experience – as if the self were locked in relation to its content. The items introduced in attempting a phenomenological description of action are then thought of as causal requisites of the actions, and the separation induces the problem of the recessive I (*ego*); whereas the items that are introduced for perception are not so readily treated as apart from the perception itself (even if it is unusual to go so far as Russell did, and identify them with perceptions). If there is a regress with perception, it is rather a regress of the objects of sight. That regress will lead to the eye's being pushed back in its turn, and so it is not inappropriate to call this the problem of the recessive eye (*oculus*). But the problem for perception crops up only because anything which is a good reason for postulating one sense datum can then seem an equally good reason for postulating another, so that for any candidate proposed as the thing perceived, we have to go back and find another candidate. Contrast that with this: for everything proposed as something acted on, we have to go back and find (not another thing acted on but) the agent's playing his role in the action.

If these remarks were to be used to criticize any rival theories, then a great deal more would need to be said about the point of view of a person as he thinks of the world affecting him, and as he thinks of himself affecting the world. We should need to understand why it can seem so hard to reconcile the point of view that people are inclined to take of their own case with the kinds of account I accept. But the remarks can suggest why my theory of action should never have seemed as attractive as the corresponding theory of perception. The sense datum theorist avoids regress simply by ruling that each visual array causes exactly one set of sense data that the mind is in touch with. In that way he retains a dualist account, but continues to think that the objects mentioned in commonplace descriptions of perceptions are causes of those perceptions. For action, though, the dualist's motivation leads to the placing of volitions behind actions, and that already makes obscure the relations between the things that follow on volitions: the events that are the effects of actions become muddled up with actions. Or, if dualism does not tempt him, then the theorist of action probably spurns all talk of conations of any kind, and forgets that our talk about trying to do things needs to be related to what we say about doing things. Either way, he is likely to pass over the option of saying that actions are things nearly all of whose commonplace descriptions introduce their effects.

4

4.1 Grice finished his paper on the causal theory of perception by putting forward tentative necessary and sufficient conditions for someone's having perceived an object. If parallelism leads anyone to suppose that what I have said about action can similarly be developed into a philosophical analysis of the concept, he will be disappointed. To indicate why my claims fall short of that will make it clearer what I have been concerned to do.

4.2 Three necessary conditions of their application display the causal character of the two concepts:

(i) There is an event of a certain kind,
(ii) there is an event of another, related kind,
(iii) the first event causes the second.

For action, events of the first sort are events of someone's trying to ϕ, and causation runs from them to events of a kind that ϕ-ing introduces. For perception, events of the second sort are (roughly) experiences as of seeing objects, and causation runs to them from events involving the objects. Neither set of conditions is sufficient for perception (Grice, 1961; Pears, 1976) or for action (Goldman, 1970; Pears, 1975), because (i) - (iii) may be satisfied (even if they are seldom actually satisfied) without the event that is an experience as of *m* (/trying to ϕ) being a perception of *m* (/action of ϕ-ing intentionally). If we were to give an analysis in either case, then at the very least we should need to find a way to say more about the kind of connection that must obtain between events or states inside a person and events or states in the world outside if the internal events are to be perceptions or actions; and certainly additional concepts from the sphere of *causation* and *explanation*, besides the extensional 'cause', would have to be employed. (See Peacocke's *differential explanation*, 1979.)

Where action is concerned, this cannot be the end of the matter. For if it is an analysis that we want, then we are bound to be discontent with an account that mentions *trying*. As soon as *trying* enters the picture, attention is confined to events that take place at and after an event that potentially initiates a chain leading away from the agent's body. But anyone who is interested in analysing *action* will need to say something about what occurs before that point. He will want to know what it is for someone to try to ϕ, and we cannot tell him much about that, except by reference to the notion of *intentionally* doing something. But in order to elucidate *intention* we must say what is distinctive about the causal history of actions. (We could use *differential explanation* again; though Peacocke's own analysis of *action* is not the two-stage affair suggested by my exposition.)

I have been anxious to separate problems about the causation of actions from problems about causation by actions. And it is no wonder if nothing positive is learnt about the causation of actions from displaying the causal character of action concepts themselves. (With perception it is rather different: an interest in the causal character of the concept is all one with an interest in how perceptions are caused.) If the hope of achieving an analysis motivates someone, then he must pass beyond the scheme used to reveal the *causation* inherent in many action concepts. As well as saying what it is for a trying to be an action, he must say what it is for states like belief and desire to issue in results in such a way that it is *via* an action (or a trying) that the result is produced. Actions will be located between mental states and events of which the subject of those states is the agent; and this will reflect the fact that actions happen where desires are translated into desired effects.

APPENDIX A
ON SOME CAUSATIVE TRANSITIVE VERBS

I claimed that 'move$_T$' belongs to a class of transitive verbs, and that it is a necessary condition of the application of any verb in that class that a sentence containing 'cause' and an intransitive verb (like 'move$_I$') be true. That was in Chapter One. In Chapter Seven I claimed that no specifically causal words besides words from the language of event causality are needed in an account of these verbs, or in an account of locutions on the pattern '*Person* cause *event*'. In this Appendix I support these claims by taking them further: I argue for a certain sort of account of causative transitive verbs in terms of their intransitive counterparts (§ 1), and I suggest that that sort of account can be used also to elucidate our talk of persons' causing things (§ 2 and § 3).

1

(A) $a\ \phi_T\ m \rightarrow m\ \phi_I$

This is the pattern of entailments distinctive of the group of verbs briefly discussed in Chapter One.

The connections here are different in kind from that between (e.g.) 'Rachel ate dinner' and 'Rachel ate', where the second sentence, though it appears to contain an intransitive 'eat', may be thought to be derived from the first simply by existential closure. Different again are verbs like 'sell'. These allow the grammatical object of the transitive to become the grammatical subject of the intransitive, and to that extent they resemble 'move$_T$' and the other instances of ϕ_T in superficial behaviour:

we have 'The new toothpaste sold', although we do not have 'Dinner ate'. Nevertheless the intransitive of 'sell' is like that of 'eat', and unlike that of 'move', inasmuch as it is still derivative from the transitive. If we hear that the new toothpaste sold (intransitive) then we understand that it must have been sold (transitive – sold by someone or ones); whereas in the cases that interest me, there appears to be no hope of founding the intransitive on the transitive.

Given the many kinds of verb that appear both transitively and intransitively, and the many categories of them (the classification here is extremely crude), it might be tempting to suggest that we give up thinking of verbs as predicates of a determinate degree (Grandy, 1975). But even if there is some truth in that suggestion, when it comes to a verb from the class to which 'move' belongs, one cannot rest content with saying that it is a unitary lexical item which, it so happens, sometimes does and sometimes does not have a grammatical object. Something more needs saying about the connection between transitive and intransitive. The entailments between the two uses are unidirectional and quite systematic, and they need explaining.

The group includes, as well as *move, melt* and *break* (and others mentioned in Chapter One), *boil, burn, burst, capsize, close, crack, dry out, freeze, halt, shut, simmer, sink, solidify, start, stop, thaw out, trip up, wake up.* And there are also examples where non-equiform words seem to be related exactly as instances of ϕ_T and ϕ_I are related – notably the pairs *raise/rise* and *kill/die.*

The use of the transitive verbs is not confined to talk of human action: lead weights sink_T corks, flames melt_T plastic, and stones break_T windows. But according to one view against which my arguments were directed, some verbs require for their analysis a certain idea of agent causality which has special consequences for human freedom. Plainly this cannot be true of verbs in all of their uses: when a lead weight is said to sink a cork its freedom is not in question. For the time being, though (until § 3), I shall follow the agent causationists at least in assuming that we have somehow singled out the occurrences of the verbs which report actions, and that we are concerned only with those.

We can begin with a particular instance of (A): 'Rupert woke_T Rachel up', and 'Rachel woke_I up'. The first sentence, we take it, reports an action; and the first entails the second. (It will usually be misleading to say that Rachel woke_I up if someone woke_T her. But it will not be false. For surely if one goes to sleep, then one is not awake again until one has woken up_I again. If anyone has doubts about whether any of the verbs I listed really do conform to (A), then he may like to reconsider the matter in the light of this point.)

Following Davidson's proposal (1967) that we should see places for events introduced by verb predicates, we have:

(1) $(\exists e)$(Woke up (Rupert, Rachel, e))
and (2) $(\exists e)$(Woke up (Rachel, e)).

The slots for events revealed here permit a very old suggestion to be cast in a new form. It has been said that 'wake up Rachel' means 'cause Rachel to wake up'. But now one can say that Rupert's waking Rachel up *is* his causing her waking up; or again, with an eye to the representations, that an event that makes (1) true causes an event that makes (2) true. So (1) can be replaced by:

(1*) $(\exists e)(\exists f)$ (Action (Rupert, e) & Cause (e, f) & Wake up (Rachel, f)).

The introduction of 'action' signals a move from *Rupert's* (*the agent's*) *causing* to *Rupert's deed's* (*the event's*) *causing*. The only novelty of the formulation is the explicit recognition of the ontology of events, and the use of 'cause' as a relation between events. I believe that this feature already avoids some of the difficulties of earlier proposals[1], and that it makes it possible to see what kind of modification to the simple claim that 'ϕ_T' means 'cause to ϕ_I' is required. There has been much criticism of that claim in the linguistics literature, and certainly a sentence like (1*) inherits some of the difficulties. But I hope it also allows us to find the remedies. So let us summarize what we have got so far in a schema, and we shall see exactly where it goes wrong.

[1] Chomsky has often objected to simple formulae like ' "wake up_T" means "cause to wake up_I" ' that in many cases 'ϕ_T' and 'cause to ϕ_I' are not even intersubstitutable *salve congruitate* (e.g. 1970, n. 31). His point is that there are constraints on what sort of word may suitably be attached to these transitive verbs so as to verify the formula. But what we have arrived at in (1*) already effects a restriction: the only sort of expression that can replace 'Rupert' there is one that designates something in the category of continuant; and the analysis does not work straightforwardly for a sentence like 'Rupert's high spirits woke up_T Rachel', which Chomsky says is less than grammatical. (This is not to suggest that only terms for continuants can fit into '— wakes up *m*'. It is just that in attempting to spell out the ties between (1) and (2), we have found a mode of representation that serves for the case where an agent is subject of the verb, and the difficulty that Chomsky noted is then evaded without arbitrary rulings.)

(B) $(\exists e)(\phi_T(a,m,e)$ iff $(\exists e)(\exists f)(\text{Action}(a,e)$ & Cause (e,f) & $\phi_I(m,f))$.

Suppose Penny orders Paul to sink a dinghy, and he obeys. Then Penny's saying what she did caused Paul's action, and Paul's action caused the dinghy to sink, so that Penny's speech act caused the sinking. But she did not sink the dinghy, and the right-to-left part of the biconditional fails. Clearly we can generate a whole series of counter-examples to the sufficiency of analyses on the pattern of (B): *a* causes *b* to cause a ϕ_I-ing of *m*; but then although both *a* and *b* satisfy '—'s action caused *m*'s ϕ_I-ing' (cp. RHS of (B)), only of *b* is it true that he ϕ_T-ed *m* (cp. LHS of (B)).

One way one might try to avoid this problem would be to deny the transitivity of 'cause'. If 'cause' is not transitive, then we cannot conclude that Penny's act caused the sinking$_I$; and the right hand side of the relevant instance of (B) is then false, as the left is. Now is it true that Penny's speech act caused the dinghy to sink? Certainly this result of applying transitivity sounds a bit odd. But plausible accounts of causation entail transitivity (see e.g. Lewis, 1973), and that is reason to deny that the oddity constitutes falsehood. Besides, the transitivity of 'cause' is actually required to make conditionals along the lines of (B) work in the host of cases where they pretheoretically seem to work, and do work. If Anna melts$_T$ the chocolate by lighting the gas, then her action causes the flame to cause the pan's heating, which, in its turn, causes the chocolate's melting$_I$. Rather than placing restrictions on transitivity, one should look for something that effects an appropriate restriction on the causes allowed in the *analysans.*[2]

Where two people each performed actions that caused the sinking of *m*, the one who sank *m* was he whose action was causally more proximate to *m*'s sinking. We can set things straight, then, by appending to the *analysans* this conjunct:

$$\ldots \& (\forall g)(\forall x)([(g \neq e) \& \text{Action}(x,g) \& \text{Cause}(g,f)] \supset \text{Cause}(g,e))).$$

[2] One way to effect the restriction is to introduce a new primitive 'CAUSE', having a sense in which '*a* CAUSED *m* to ϕ_I' is true just in case *a* ϕ_T-ed *m*. (See McCawley (1968).) And someone may argue that this 'CAUSE' corresponds to a (silent) morpheme of English. But if we are interested in the analysis of these verbs, then even if we were persuaded of the existence of this morpheme, we should still want to know whether its meaning can be given in terms of the ordinary (audible) words of English.

Any action that caused *m*'s sinking, except for *a*'s action, caused *a*'s action.

To see how this works, imagine that Penny is *a* in the case where she orders Paul to sink the dinghy. Well, then the new right hand says that any action other than Penny's which caused the sinking caused her action. But Paul's action though it caused the sinking did not cause Penny's action; so, like the left, the new right hand side is now false.

It is worth noticing that there need not be two persons involved for the problem with (B) to arise. Suppose someone locks himself out of his house, and has to break a window in order to re-enter. His locking himself out causes, in due course, the window's breaking. But his locking himself out is not his breaking the window. My solution covers this case: with the new addition to the analysis only his later action, say throwing a stone at the window pane, will count as a breaking$_T$. Thus:

(C) $(\exists e)(\phi_T(a,m,e))$ iff $(\exists e)(\exists f)$ (Action(a,e) & Cause(e,f) & $\phi_T(m,f)$ & $(\forall x)(\forall g)([(g \neq e)$ & Action (x,g) & Cause$(g,f)] \supset$ Cause$(g,e)))$.

2

Let the added conjunct seem *ad hoc*, let me show that the complex predicate uncovered in the analysis has another use. Consider the expression 'the cause of *a*', where *a* is an event and the whole expression denotes an agent. Even when many people are causally related to an event through their actions, we very often take it that just one of them is *the* cause. So uniqueness of denotation for that expression needs to be semantically guaranteed. But *the* cause of *a* is surely the one, among those who cause *a*, who causes an event closest *a*. Thus 'the cause of *a* is P' could be represented:

(*) $(\exists x)(\exists e)($Action(x,e) & Cause(e,a) & $(\forall y)(\forall f)(($Action(y,f) & $(f \neq e)$ & Cause$(f,a)) \supset$ Cause$(f,e))$ & P$(x))$.

And if this is right, then (C) boils down to this:

(D) a ϕ_T-s m iff a is the cause of m's ϕ_I-ing.

It will be worth connecting 'the cause of *a*' as that expression applies to agents with uses of 'the cause' that apply to events. It is much easier to say how we hit upon one person as the cause than it is to say how we single out from all the candidates an answer to the question *Which event was the cause*?. If 'cause' is transitive, then it will often be true to say of any one of a large number of events that it caused a (and even if we have chosen one, there will always be a vast number of ways we could have elected to describe it, Davidson (1967b)). One of the principles that we employ in practice and that relates to present concerns has been spelt out by Hart and Honoré:

> A deliberate human act is . . . most often a barrier and a goal in tracing back causes . . . : it is something *through* which we do not trace the cause of a later event and something *to* which we do trace the cause through intervening causes of other kinds (1959, p. 41).

In other words, we are apt to cite as 'the' cause the event that is the relevant action of whatever person was *the cause* in the sense explicated in (*) (and to describe it as an action). Still, as Hart and Honoré themselves say, there will often be more than one perfectly correct answer to a question about what event is the cause. And, as has often been remarked, which answers are acceptable depends very much upon the interests of the investigator.

The talk of relativity of interests is vague, admittedly. But it combines with Hart and Honoré's idea of tracing back to suggest a partial account of why we seem not to allow wholesale transitivity to 'cause', of why we may be reluctant to say, for example, that Penny's speech act caused the sinking, even though it caused something that caused the sinking. If an investigator brings a particular set of concerns to some causal enquiry, then he looks for an answer to the question 'What event was the cause of a?' which stays as close to a as is compatible with his engaging with one of his concerns. And if in tracing back we arrive at a point at which, whatever conceivable interest was in question, the cause relative to that interest has already been passed, then we shall be reluctant to say that events still further back are causes at all. In the case of the dinghy's sinking, without more details of the story, it is hard to imagine any interest there might be except the common human one. Thus not only is Paul's action called *the* cause of the sinking$_I$, but also Penny's earlier action is unlikely to be cited as *a* cause. And generally, because there are limits on the causally related events that we are prepared to say caused any event, transitivity of 'cause' *seems* to have its limits.

But we are less reluctant to call Penny herself a cause than we are to call her action a cause. This too is not surprising. When persons, not events, are candidates for causes, there would be no difference in the use made of the ideas of a person's being *a cause* and of her being *the cause*, if we could not trace back through actions. And of course it is the difference there is between *a cause* and *the cause* which enables us, in the analysis (C), to focus upon those causers of ϕ_I-ings who are subjects of ϕ_T.

Still, it may be that there are limits on the tracing back of causes even where causation by persons is our interest. Perhaps one cannot be too remote from an event and still be said to have caused it, or too remote from something's sinking_I and still be said to have sunk it. If so, there will be a fault in my account of 'person is the cause' and of the transitive verbs. The truth, I suspect, is that we do not have firm intuitions about the sorts of example that are at issue here. If someone triggers a causal chain that terminates at length in a dinghy's sinking, then it may be quite unclear whether he has sunk the dinghy or not. At any rate, I shall not try to place further qualifications on what must be true of an action that causes a sinking_I of x for the agent to have sunk_T x.

Fodor (1976, p. 130n.) denies that there could be any account of these transitive verbs, and claims that we can only say what they mean by using them. He may be right in that. But provided that my attempt at an analysis is on the right lines, the claim that I exploited throughout the essay – that a person's action of ϕ_T-ing may be identified with an event that causes a ϕ_I-ing – stands firm.

Johnson (1972) gives a number of examples that would count against (B) above, but not, I think, against (C). He concludes that 'we should be wary of identifying a causing act with a killing (generally – a causing act with a ϕ_T-ing)'. But if his examples leave (C) unscathed, then we have not been provided with any reason to be especially wary of making such identifications. To disprove identities between actions of killings and events that cause death (to disprove that every killing is the same as some event that causes a death), it would have to be shown that there are failures of necessity, not merely failures of sufficiency, in analyses like (B) and (C). And so far as I know, no one has ever claimed to have shown that.

3

It is time to heed the fact that individuals other than persons or events can cause things, and to recognize too that persons may cause more than their actions cause, so that they can truly be said to have woken$_T$ others, broken$_T$ windows or closed$_T$ doors, without having behaved as intentional agents in their wakings$_T$, breakings$_T$ or closings$_T$. Suppose, for instance, that Mary deliberately pushes a passive Matthew, and that he closes$_T$ a door simply through being pushed. No action of his caused its closing.

The need to accommodate such examples may encourage the response that it was wrong ever to start with the word 'action' in a proposed analysis, a more neutral word for relating Substances to Events should have been used instead – say 'participate'. Persons who have behaved as agents could still sometimes satisfy the relevant formulae, because persons participate in their actions.

This proposal would enable us to see how it is that Matthew closed$_T$ the door in the case described. What it fails to allow for, however, is that Mary can also be said to have closed it there: closing the door was something she did by pushing Matthew. It is instructive to compare this case with one of the type that was the basis of discussion in § 1. Suppose Mary's part in getting the door closed consisted in persuading Matthew to close it. Here, although Mary initiates a causal sequence that results in the door's coming to be closed, Matthew's role is that of intentional agent. And here, but not in the previous case, Mary would not be said to have closed it at all.

Provided that (C) is read as we have it, with the word 'action' throughout, both Mary's action in the first case, where she pushes Matthew, and Matthew's action in the second case, where Mary persuades him, will be shown to be the closings$_T$ they are. But unless we say that 'action' occurs throughout, we cannot explain how it is that *Mary* closed the door in the one case, but not in the other. And unless we allow in addition that there is something like (C), but with 'participate' replacing 'action' throughout, we cannot explain how it is that Matthew closed the door at all where he was pushed. (Note that if (C) is read with a word like 'participate' throughout, there are parallel cases that justify the conjunct that was added to set things straight before. A bat's movement causes the movement of a ball which in turn causes a window to break. Then though perhaps misleading, it is true to say that the movement of the bat caused the window's breaking$_I$. But by the modified version of (C) [substituting 'participate' for 'action'], it was the ball that broke$_T$ the window; and this is the right result.)

What this points to is a real ambiguity in the transitive verbs themselves. We should distinguish systematically between two words either of which may figure on the right of (C): 'action', and some other word that does not invoke the idea of human agency.

Similar examples could be used to argue for an analogous ambiguity in '—— was the cause of'. And there is a number of more or less explicity causal constructions that can take either terms for events or terms for persons as subjects. As well as the simple 'cause', we have 'bring *e* about', 'bring it about that *p*' and 'make *m* (be) F'. And I take it that we can give accounts of all these locutions using the relation 'cause' between events and either the word 'action' or 'participate'. Wherever the name of a person is the subject of the verb, both accounts will apply. So, for example, 'Person *a* caused *a*' may mean *(∃e)(Action(a,e) & Cause(e,a)),* or, merely, *(∃e)(Participate(a,e) & Cause(e,a)).*

If this is right, then it is a partial vindication of Chisholm, who thought that 'Person caused . . . ' locutions brought the notion of agency with them (cp. Chapter Seven, 3.2). But it is not (as Chisholm may have thought) that, as soon as we find one of these constructions attached to the name of a person, the role of agent has automatically been conferred upon the person named, only that there is a sense of each in which a sentence containing it has to be verified by a doing that was a doing of something intentionally done. To account for that sense, we do not need any special notion of causation. The idea of something's being related to an event as an agent is related to his action will explain all the uses of 'cause' that impute agency.

APPENDIX B
LOGICAL FORM, EVENT INDIVIDUATION

Arguments for the account of action individuation I defend might have proceeded from a thesis about the logical form of action sentences, or from a general account of the individuation of events. I have not followed either procedure, but wish to note what I take myself to be committed to on these two issues.

1

In (1967a) Davidson proposed that certain adverbially modified action sentences have the logical form of an existentially quantified conjunction. E.g.

$$(\exists e)(\text{Walk}(\text{John},e)\ \&\ \text{In}(\text{the park},e)\ \&\ \text{At}(\text{midnight},e)).$$

We can perhaps separate out two parts of his proposal: (i) that some verbs are satisfied only if there is an event of some sort, and (ii) that some adverbs are predicates of events. And we might say that the first is a thesis about the *ontology* of even the very simplest action sentences (like 'John walked'), and the second a (not independent) thesis about the *structure* of some of the slightly more complicated ones (like 'John walked in the park').

Some of my arguments about actions depend crucially upon the need to make sense of what we say when we use nominal expressions that appear to denote events, and when we link those expressions with sentences that appear to report actions. If we take it that the relation between 'John's signalling' and 'John signalled' is such that the sentences

'There was at least one signalling by John' and 'John signalled' are equivalent (cp. Appendix to Chapter One), and if we think that that equivalence shows that one who asserts either sentence is committed to the existence of an event, then, if it is granted that any representation of sentences designed for use in a theory of meaning must reflect all the ontological commitments of speakers, we must accept Davidson's (i).

The claimed equivalence of sentences containing nominals with sentences containing verbs cannot bear the load it carries in this argument, unless we have reason to think that a nominal like 'John's signalling' has more than the *appearance* of denoting, and that 'There was a signalling' is *genuinely* existential. I do not know how to prove that there are events, but I hope to have made it seem plausible by demonstrating that our understanding of action is increased when we speak explicitly as if there were events. To take a single example: If we accept that anyone who ϕ-s intentionally tries to ϕ, there is a further question how someone's ϕ-ing intentionally and his trying to ϕ are related (by identity, as part to whole, as cause to effect?). This further question needs an answer. But it cannot be asked without talking about events. I suppose that someone might say that it was merely a part of the project of philosophical analysis to answer this question, and that it is only philosophers who need to regard action sentences as reporting particulars. Then he could accept the claims of the essay, but reject all of Davidson's theses about ontology and logical form.[1]

Although the claim about ontology may receive further support from considerations about the structure of action sentences themselves, it is made here quite independently of determining whether any adverb is a predicate or a predicate modifier.[2] The details of the structure of action sentences will depend upon how we treat quantifiers (whether we think that the existential quantifier automatically introduces conjunction, for instance – cp. Wiggins, 1979), and upon some general questions about which modes of semantic combination most faithfully account for our ways of speaking both about continuants and about events.

But there is a further question for me about ontology and structure. I have claimed that if ever there is an action of any kind, then there are two events – the action and an effect of a sort without which the action wouldn't be an action of the kind it is. Does this mean that the logical form of action sentences is even more complex than Davidson allowed, and that we shall find two existential quantifiers at the beginning of any representation of an action sentence? Well, some action verbs may carry that sort of complexity.[3] But there is no mechanical way of pairing an arbitrary action verb with a description of an event (of 'an effect introduced') such that we can say that the original action verb is satisfied only if there was such an event (cp. Davidson, 1967a, p. 119 last para.).[4] Consider 'He walked'. Apparently we cannot decompose 'walk' into two predicates, one applicable to an action, and another applicable to an event (caused by his action) which occurred if and only if he walked; and it seems clear that 'walk' must be treated as a simple verb by a theory of meaning.[5] Note, however, that to show that my account of action applies to actions of people walking would not require any claim about the analysis of 'walk', let alone a claim about a complexity in the logical form of sentences containing 'walk'. I need only say that if a person walks, then he moves_T a part of his body in some way or other, and that his movements_T constitute his walking.

2

The argument of Chapter Two, § 2.2 assumes that *e* and *f* are distinct if they have different causal relata. This is, as it were, the trivial (Leibnizian) half of Davidson's criterion of event individuation (1969a). Although I nowhere argue from the other half – that no two events can have the same causes and effects – , I do in fact accept it. (Critics typically complain that it does not supply an effective method for settling identity questions, and then ignore the important question whether it is true.)

Acceptance of Davidson's criterion as stating a necessary truth about events does not commit one to any view about their necessary, or essential, properties.[6] This is just as well, because the argument of Chapter Three, § 3.3 relies upon finding intelligible the idea that an event might still have existed even if it had not had the effects that it actually did. (A version of the necessity of origin for events would say that they must have the causes they actually do, which seems to me less implausible than the parallel essentialist claim about effects.)

1 What this person cannot do is propose some rival ontology at this point. Barry Taylor's (1976) states of affairs, for example, (though they may have many uses) cannot be used to say what the speakers of action sentences commit themselves to, *if* we think that what they commit themselves to can be picked out using certain verb

nominalizations. The problem is that what is true of any of the descripta that Taylor assigns to sentences, and derivatively to the nominalizations, is not what is true of e.g. someone's raising his arm.
(a) Sets are not the sorts of things to have the properties that the things denoted by the event terms of our language have; and vice versa. No set is located in any bathroom, for instance; and nothing that happened on Tuesday is a member of anything that happened on Wednesday.
(b) Even if their identification with sets could somehow be eliminated, Taylor's events would still have only such properties as are conferred on them by the particular words used to describe them. Unlike the things that our event terms denote, they are not things about which more and more can always be learned.

2 Sometimes the controversy between Davidson and others is set up as if certain adverbs had to be *either* modifiers of predicates that aren't predicates of events *or* predicates of events. But one group of expressions that we can argue must be treated as *modifiers of predicates of events* is the group of 'by'-phrases. (As *modifiers* for reasons advanced in Chapter One, § 2.4, as modifiers of *event* predicates because otherwise we cannot so much as formulate the claim people make when they say that 'by' is asymmetrical, cp. p. 93, note 2.

3 Some of the claims about causative verbs that are used by Generative Semanticists to support their position might be used in the present framework to argue that e.g. 'move$_T$' is a four-place predicate, with places for agent, patient, causing event and caused event. But note that the account of verbs like 'move$_T$' given in Appendix A says nothing about the logical form of sentences containing them.

4 One proposal for a mechanical way of pairing (which would have application only for transitive verbs) is that the passivized nominal always gives a description of an effect of any action described by the active form, so that e.g. an event of B's being shot is an event that an action of A must have caused if A shot B. (I note that B's being shot seems a much better candidate than B's being shot by A. But I find that too hard to explain to wish to put any weight on it.)

David Pears has suggested it as a possible objection to me that 'his finger's being moved$_T$ (by him?)' both denotes the same events as 'his moving$_T$ his finger' and denotes events that occur specifically where his finger is, contrary to the claims of Chapter One. But if the proposal about active and passive is right, it supplies an answer to this objection: 'his finger's being moved$_T$' actually picks out his finger's moving$_I$. I do not know whether the proposal is right, but would make two other points in reply to the objection. (i) Switching to an example where theory may not have warped my intuitions, I find that my uncertainty about where the glass's being broken happened, in a case when someone broke a glass by throwing something at it, is wholly dependent upon my uncertainty about what is meant by 'the glass's being broken'. Thus I doubt whether we can take any of these passive descriptions and start with the conviction *both* that the description picks out an action *and* that it picks out something that happened where the patient is. (ii) 'His finger's being caused to move' seems quite as problematic as 'his finger's being moved'; and if it is, then the objection can hardly be used to argue for the identity of movings$_T$ and movings$_I$, as against the claim that movings$_T$ cause movings$_I$.

5 This point shows that some of my talk of describing actions 'in terms' of effects is less than accurate. And it shows that there is sometimes indeterminacy in the notion of 'the' effect introduced by an ⟨action, description⟩ pair. This may make for an indeterminacy in the notion of basic$_C$ (but it need not, because it could be indeterminate exactly what events are introduced by an ⟨action, description⟩ pair, but quite determinate whether 'the' event introduced by one pair is causally prior to 'the' event introduced by some other pair).

6 *Pace* e.g. Platts, 1979, p. 205. Compare the obviously fallacious step FROM Necessarily no two material things of kind *K* can be in the same place at the same time TO if *x* is of *K* and is at P at *t*, then at *t*, *x* has to be at P.

BIBLIOGRAPHY*

Abbreviations for journal references

A	*Analysis*
AJP	*Australisian Journal of Philosophy*
APQ	*American Philosophical Quarterly*
C	*Critica*
CJP	*Canadian Journal of Philosophy*
E	*Erkenntnis*
I	*Inquiry*
JP	*Journal of Philosophy*
LI	*Linguistic Inquiry*
M	*Mind*
N	*Nous*
P	*Philosophy*
PR	*Philosophical Review*
PAS/S	*Proceedings of the Aristotelian Society /Supplementary Volume*
S	*Synthèse*

Annas, Julia (1978), 'How Basic are Basic Actions?', *PAS*, LXXXVII, 195–213.

Anscombe, G. E. M. (1957), *Intention* (Oxford: Blackwell).

Austin, J. L. (1956), 'A Plea for Excuses', in *Philosophical Papers* (Oxford: Clarendon, 1970); originally in *PAS* LVIII, 1–30.

Austin, John, *The Province of Jurisprudence Determined*, with an Introduction by H. L. A. Hart (London: Weidenfeld & Nicolson, 1954).

Baier, Annette (1971), 'The Search for Basic Actions', *APQ*, VIII, 161–170.

* Only works cited in the text appear here.

Beardsley, Monroe (1975), 'Actions and Events: the Problem of Individuation', *APQ*, XII, 263–76.

Bennett, Jonathan (1971), *Locke, Berkeley, Hume* (Oxford: Clarendon).

Bennett, Jonathan (1973), 'Shooting, Killing and Dying', *CJP*, II, 315–24.

Bentham, Jeremy, *Introduction to the Principles of Morals and Legislation*, edited by J.H. Barnes and H. L. A. Hart (London; Athlone Press, 1970).

Berkeley, George, *The Principles of Human Knowledge* and *Three Dialogues Between Hylas and Philonous,* vol. II of *The Works,* edited by A. A. Luce and T. E. Jessop (London: Nelson, 1949).

Binkley, Robert (1976), 'The Logic of Action', in Brand and Walton (1976), 87–104.

Brand, Myles (1968), 'Danto on Basic Actions', *N*, 2, 187–90.

Brand, M. and Walton, D. (eds) (1976), *Action Theory* (Dordrecht: D. Reidel).

Brown, D. G. (1968), *Action* (Toronto University Press).

Chisholm, Roderick M. (1966), 'Freedom and Action', in Lehrer (1966), 11–44.

Chisholm, Roderick M. (1976a), *Person and Object* (London: Allen & *Logical Way of Doing Things*, edited by K. Lambert (New Haven and London: Yale University Press).

Chisholm, Roderick M. (1976a), *Person and Object* (London: Allen & Unwin).

Chisholm, Roderick M. (1976b), 'The Agent as Cause', in Brand and Walton (1976), 199–212.

Chomsky, N. (1970), 'Remarks on Nominalization', in *Readings in English Transformational Grammar*, edited by R. A. Jacobs and J. S. Rosenbaum (London: Ginn).

Collingwood, R. G. (1940), *Philosophical Essays*, Vol. II (Oxford: Clarendon).

Danto, Arthur (1963), 'What We Can Do', *JP*, LX, 434–45.

Danto, Arthur (1965), 'Basic Actions', *APQ*, II, 108–25.

Danto, Arthur (1966), 'Freedom and Forbearance', in Lehrer (1966), 45–63.

Danto, Arthur (1973), *Analytical Philosophy of Action* (Cambridge University Press).

D'Arcy, Eric (1963), *Human Acts: An Essay in Their Moral Evaluation* (Oxford: Clarendon).

Davidson, Donald (1963), 'Actions, Reasons and Causes', *JP*, LX, 685–700.

Davidson, Donald (1967a), 'The Logical Form of Action Sentences', in *The Logic of Decision and Action*, edited by N. Rescher (Dordrecht: D. Reidel), 87–95 and 115–20.

Davidson, Donald (1967b), 'Causal Relations', *JP*, LXIV, 691–703.

Davidson, Donald (1969a), 'The Individuation of Events', in *Essays in Honour of Carl G. Hempel*, edited by N. Rescher (Dordrecht: Reidel), 216–34.

Davidson, Donald (1969b), 'On Events and Event Descriptions', in *Fact and Existence*, edited by J. Margolis (Oxford: Blackwell), 74–84.

Davidson, Donald (1970), 'Mental Events', in *Experience and Theory* edited by Lawrence Foster and J. W. Swanson (Amherst: University of Massachusetts Press), 79–101.

Davidson, Donald (1971a), 'Agency', in *Agent, Action and Reason*, edited by R. Binkley *et al.* (Toronto University Press).

Davidson, Donald (1971b), 'Eternal vs. Ephemeral Events', *N* 5, 335–49.

Davidson, Donald (1972), 'Freedom to Act', in *Essays on Freedom of Action*, edited by T. Honderich (London: Routledge & Kegan Paul, 1973), 139–56.

Davidson, Donald (1973), 'The Material Mind', in *Logic, Methodology and the Philosophy of Science*, vol. IV edited by P. Suppes *et al.* (Amsterdam: North Holland).

Davidson, Donald (1976), 'Hempel on Explaining Action', *E*, 10, 239–53.

Davis, Lawrence H. (1979), *Theory of Action* (Englewood Cliffs, N. J.: Prentice Hall).

Descartes, R. *Philosophical Letters*, translated and edited by Anthony Kenny (Oxford: Clarendon, 1970).

Donagan, Alan (1977), 'Chisholm's Theory of Agency', *JP*, LXXIV, 692–703.

Donnellan, Keith S. (1963), 'Knowing What I Am Doing', *JP*, LX, 401–9.

Fodor, J. J. (1976), *The Language of Thought* (Sussex: Harvester Press).

Foley, Richard (1977), 'Deliberate Action', *PR*, LXXXVI, 58–69.

Gasking, D. (1955), 'Causation and Recipes', *M*, LXIV, 479–87.

Goldman, Alvin I. (1970), *A Theory of Human Action* (Englewood Cliffs, N. J.: Prentice Hall).

Goldman, Alvin I. (1971), 'The Individuation of Action', *JP*, LXVIII 761–74.

Goldman, Alvin I. (1976), 'The Volitional Theory Revisited', in Brand and Walton (1976), 67–85.

Grandy, Richard I. (1975), 'Anadic Logic and English', *S*, 32, 395–402.

Grice, H. P. (1961), 'The Causal Theory of Perception', *PASS*, XXXV, 121–52.

Grice, H. P. (1971), 'Intention and Uncertainty', *Proceedings of the British Academy*.

Grice, H. P. (1975), 'Logic and Conversation', in *The Logic of Grammar*, edited by D. Davidson and G. Harman (Encinco, Cal.: Dickenson).

Hamilton, W. *Lectures on Metaphysics and Logic*, vol. I, edited by H. L. Mansel and John Veitch (London: Blackwood & Sons 1870).

Harman, G. (1973), *Thought* (Princeton University Press).

Hart, H. L. A. and Honoré, A. M. (1959), *Causation in the Law* (Oxford: Clarendon).

Hobbes, T., *Leviathan* edited by C. B. Macpherson, (Harmondsworth: Penguin, 1968).

Hopkins, James (1978), 'Mental States, Natural Kinds and Psychophysical Laws, *PASS*, LII, 221–36.

Hornsby, Jennifer (1979), 'Actions and Identities', *A*, 39.

Hornsby, Jennifer (1980), 'Arm Raising and Arm Rising', *P*, 55.

Hume, D., *Enquiry Concerning Human Understanding* and *A Treatise of Human Nature* see vols. I–IV of *The Philosophical Works*, edited by Selby-Bigge; London: Oxford University Press, 1975).

James, William (1890), *Principles of Psychology*, (authorized edition in two unabridged volumes, New York: Dover, 1950).

Johnson, Conrad D. (1972), 'Davidson on Primitive Actions that Cause Deaths', *A*, 33, 36–41.

Kenny, Anthony (1963), *Action, Emotion and Will* (London: Routledge & Kegan Paul).

Kenny, Anthony (1976), *Will, Freedom and Power* (London: Routledge & Kegan Paul).

Kim, Jaegwon (1974), 'Non-Causal Connexions', *N*, 8, 41–52.

Lehrer, Keith (ed.) (1966), *Freedom and Determinism* (New York: Random House).

Lewis, David (1973), 'Causation', *JP*, LXX, 556–67.

Locke, Don (1974), 'Action, Movement and Neurophysiology', *I*, 17, 23–42.

Locke, John, *The Works of John Locke* (London 1812).

Mackie, J. L. (1974), *The Cement of the Universe* (Oxford: Clarendon).

Mackie, J. L. (1976), 'Review of Georg Henrik Von Wright: *Causation and Determinism*', *JP*, LXXIII, 213–18.

McCann, Hugh (1974), 'Volition and Basic Action', *PR*, LXXXIII, 451–73.

McCawley, James (1968), 'Lexical Insertion in a Transformational Grammar without Deep Structure', *Papers of the Chicago Linguistics Society*.

Melden, A. I. (1956), 'Action', *PR*, LXV, 523–41.

Melden, A. I. (1960), 'Willing', *PR*, LXIX, 475–84.

Melden, A. I. (1961), *Free Action* (London: Humanities Press).

Mill, John Stuart (1814), *Logic* (New York).

Miller, Jonathan (1978), *The Body in Question* (London: Jonathan Cape).

Montmarquet, James, A. (1978), 'Actions and Bodily Movements', *A*, 38, 137–40.

Nagel, T. (1969), 'The Boundaries of Inner Space', *JP*, LXVI, 452–8.

O'Shaughnessy, Brian (1963), 'Observation and the Will', *JP*, LX, 367–92.

O'Shaughnessy, Brian (1974), 'Trying (as the Mental "Pineal Gland")', *JP*, LXXI, 365–86.

Peacocke, Christopher (1979), *Holistic Explanation: Action, Space, Interpretation* (Oxford University Press).

Pears, D. F. (ed.) (1963), *Freedom and The Will* (London: Macmillan).

Pears, D. F. (1975), 'The Appropriate Causation of Intentional Basic Actions', *C*, VII, 39–69.

Pears, D. F. (1976), 'The Causal Conditions of Perception', *S*, 33, 25–40.

Platts, Mark de B. (1979), *Ways of Meaning* (London: Routledge & Kegan Paul).

Prichard, H. (1932), 'Duty and Ignorance of Fact', in Prichard (1949), 18–39.

Prichard, H. (1945), 'Acting, Willing, Desiring', in Prichard (1949), 187–98.

Prichard, H. (1949), *Moral Obligation* (Oxford: Clarendon).

Quinton, A. M. (1955), 'The Problem of Perception', *M*, LXIV, 28–51.

Reid, Thomas, *Essays on the Active Powers of the Human Mind*, edited by B. A. Brody (Cambridge, Mass: MIT Press, 1969).

Russell, Bertrand (1927), *An Outline of Philosophy* (London: Allen & Unwin).

Russell, Bertrand (1940; 1962), *An Enquiry into Meaning and Truth* (London: Allen & Unwin; Harmondsworth: Penguin).

Ryle, G. (1949; 1970), *The Concept of Mind* (London: Hutchinson; Harmondsworth: Penguin, page refs. to Penguin edition).

Sellars, Wilfrid (1966), 'Thought and Action', in Lehrer (1966), 141–74.

Sellars, Wilfrid, (1976), 'Volitions Re-affirmed', in Brand and Walton (1976), 47–66.

Shwayder, David (1965), *The Stratification of Behaviour* (London: Routledge & Kegan Paul).

Silber, R. (1964), 'Human Action and the Language of Volitions', *PAS*, LXIV, 199–220.

Smith, Carlota (1972), 'On Causative Verbs and Derived Nominals in English', *LI*, 3, i, 136–8.

Stoutland, Frederick (1968), 'Basic Actions and Causality', *JP*, LXV, 467–75.

Strawson, P. F. (1963), Discussion in Pears (1963).

Strawson, P. F. (1974), 'Causation in Perception', in *Freedom and Resentment* (London: Methuen).

Taylor, Barry (1976), 'States of Affairs', in *Truth and Meaning*, edited by G. Evans and J. McDowell (Oxford: Clarendon).

Taylor, Richard (1966), *Action and Purpose* (Englewood Cliffs, N.J.: Prentice Hall).

Thalberg, Irving (1962), 'Intending the Impossible', *AJP*, 40, 49–56.

Thalberg, Irving (1971), 'Singling Out Actions, their Properties and Components', *JP*, LXVIII, 781–6.

Thalberg, Irving (1977), *Perception, Emotion and Action: A Component Approach* (Oxford: Blackwell).

Thalberg, Irving (1978), 'The Irreducibility of Events', *A*, 38, 1–9.

Thomson, J. Jarvis (1971a), 'The Time of a Killing', *JP*, LXVIII, 115–32.

Thomson, J. Jarvis (1971b), 'Individuating Actions', *JP*, LXVIII, 774–81.

Thomson, J. Jarvis, (1977), *Acts and Other Events* (Ithaca, N.Y.: Cornell University Press).

Vesey, G. (1961), 'Volition', *P*, 36, 325–65.

Warnock, Mary (1963), Participant in discussion in Pears (1963).

Wiggins, David (1979), ' "Most" and "All" ', in *Reference, Truth and Reality* edited by M. de B. Platts (London: Routledge & Kegan Paul).

Wilkins, John (1668), *An Essay Towards a Real Character, and a Philosophical Language* (London: printed for Sa. Gellibrand).

Williams, Bernard (1978), *Descartes* (Harmondsworth, Penguin).

Wittgenstein, Ludwig, *Tractatus-Logico-Philosophicus* (London: Routledge & Kegan Paul, 1922).

Wittgenstein, Ludwig, *Philosophical Investigations*, translated by G. E. M. Anscombe (Oxford: Blackwell, 1953).

Wittgenstein, Ludwig, *Zettel*, edited by G. E. M. Anscombe and G. H. von Wright (Oxford: Blackwell, 1967).

Wright, G. H. von (1971), *Explanation and Understanding* (London: Routledge & Kegan Paul).

Wright, G. H. von (1973), 'On the Logic and Epistemology of the Causal Relation', in *Logic, Methodology and Philosophy of Science Vol. IV*, edited by P. Suppes *et al.* (Amsterdam: North Holland), 293–312.

Wright, G. H. von (1974), *Causality and Determinism* (New York and London: Columbia University Press).

Wright, Larry (1974), 'Emergency Behaviour', *I*, 17, 43–7.

INDEX

Ability, 84, 95
Actionist theory, 89–92
Agent causation, 15n., 53, 55, 89–90, 96–101, 125, 132
Annas, Julia, 79, 138
Anscombe, G. E. M., 6, 7, 107–10, 138
"Asymmetry" of 'by', 7–8, 93–4
Asymmetry of 'cause', 90–3
Attempts, *see* trying
Austin, J. L., 90, 138
Austin, John, 47, 138

Backwards causation, 21–2, 25, 27, 28, 92–3
Baier, Annette, 12, 66, 68, 79, 138
$Basic_C$: defined, 70–1
Basic*: defined, 73
BASIC: defined, 78–9
Basic action, 15, 20, 33, 66–88, 104; *see also* causal –, compositional –, preparatory –, teleological –
Basmajian, 86
Beardsley, Monroe, 29, 138
Belief, 41, 79–81, 83–4
Bennett, Jonathan, 9, 52, 138
Bentham, Jeremy, 47, 48, 54, 138
Berkeley, George, 47, 48, 52, 56, 62, 138
Binkley, Robert, 47, 138
Biofeedback, 86
Bodily movements, *see* $movements_T$ and $movements_I$
Brand, Myles, 67, 139
Brown, D. G., 56, 139
'By', 6–8, 27–8, 38, 60–1, 72–7, 83, 90–3

Causal basicness, 68, 70–2, 74–6, 104
Causal priority, *see* asymmetry of 'cause'
Causative verbs, 13–4, 124–32, 134, 136n.3
Chisholm, Roderick M., 15n., 47, 89–90, 96–9, 101, 132, 139
Chomsky, N., 126n., 139
Collingwood, R. G., 90, 99–100, 139
Component approach, 29–30
Compositional basicness, 68, 80, 85
Conations: defined, 47; *see also* setting oneself to, trying, volition, willing
Control, 85–6
Counting actions, 29, 80n.

Danto, Arthur, 39, 49, 53, 57–9, 77, 79, 139
D'Arcy, Eric, 6, 139
Davidson, Donald, vii, 4, 6, 7, 9, 10, 11, 12, 20, 31, 36, 39, 79, 126, 129, 133–5, 136, 139–40
Davis, Lawrence, H., 31–2, 42, 47, 62, 140
Dependence, 67, 77, 95
Descartes, R., 47, 48, 58, 59, 140
Desires, 56–7, 79–81
Determinism, 96
"Doing *x*", 4, 8, 52, 55, 120
Doings and things done, 4, 6, 8n., 11, 16, 69, 120
Donagan, Alan, 98n., 140
Donnellan, Keith, 108, 140
Dualism, 56, 57–60, 119–22

Event ontology, 3, 19, 31–2, 133–4, 135–6

Fine, Kit, 8n.
Fodor, Jerry, 130, 140
Foley, Richard, 47, 62, 140
Freedom, 95–7, 125

Gasking, D., 90, 140
"Generation", 68, 75
Generative semantics, 136n.3
"Generic" events, 91n., 98n., 135–6n.
Goldman, Alvin I., 5, 7, 16–9, 31, 54–5, 67, 68, 75, 79, 123, 140
Grandy, Richard E., 125, 140
Grice, H. P., 34, 87, 111–14, 115, 116, 123, 140

Hamilton, William, 47, 140
Harman, Gilbert, 35, 140
Hart, H. L. A., 129, 140
Hobbes, T., 47, 48, 140
Honoré, A. M., 129, 140
Hopkins, James, 78n., 81, 141
Hume, David, 40, 47, 51, 121, 141

Identities: between actions, 6–10, 18–9, 29–32; between actions and neurophysiological events, 13n., 105–6; between actions and tryings, 38, 45; between tryings, 39
Individuation: of actions, 6–11, 16–9, 29–32, 67; of events generally, 135, 137n.6
Infinite regress, *see* regress arguments
Intention, 26, 54, 81, 94–5
'Intentionally', 36–7, 39, 43n., 45, 65n., 78, 79–81, 83
Introduced effects: defined, 70
Irreducibility, 96–7, 105

James, William, 40, 140
Johnson, Conrad D., 130, 140

Kenny, Anthony, 49, 141
Kim, Jaegwon, 77, 141
Kinaesthetic sensations, 44, 108–9
Knowing how to and knowing that, 83–4, 88
Knowledge, 35–6, 83, 84, 85–7, 115–17; and trying, 34–6, 40–1, 44, 58, 116; of one's own actions, 42, 44, 107–10, 116; of others' actions, 102–7, 117; without observation, 107–8

Landry's patient, 40, 41–4, 108–10
Lewis, David, 77, 127, 141
Locke, Don, 37n., 141
Locke, John, 46, 47, 48, 51, 55–8, 108, 141
Logical connection argument, 62
Logical form, 4, 133–5, 136n.3

Mackie, J. L., 92, 96n., 141
McCann, Hugh, 47, 62, 141
McCawley, James, 127n., 141
McCulloch, Gregory, 64–5n.
Manipulability theory, *see* actionist theory

Means/end, 75, 79–80
Melden, A. I., 12, 50, 141
Mill, James Stuart, 47, 48, 141
Miller, Jonathan, 13n., 141
Montmarquet, James, A., 53, 141
'Move', 2–3, 10, 13, 124–5
Movements$_T$ and movements$_I$, 2–3, 5, 10–11, 50–51, 55, 57, 98, 120
Muscle contractions, 20–8, 78n., 86–7, 93–4

Nagel, Thomas, 86, 141
Nominals, 2, 4n., 16, 17, 133–4, 136n.4

Objects of conations, 54–5, 63
O'Shaughnessy, Brian, 34, 27n., 107n., 141

Passives, 136n.4
Peacocke, Christopher, 78n., 123, 141
Pears, David, vii, 67, 123, 136n.4, 141–2
Perception, 111–23
"Perform an action", 8n., 120
Platts, Mark de B., 137n.6, 142
Preparatory basicness, 68, 78n., 80
Prichard, H., 14, 15, 46, 47, 48, 60–3, 66, 108, 142

Quinton, A. M., 114–15, 142

Regress arguments, 48–50, 63–5, 88, 101, 117–18, 120–1
Reid, Thomas, 47, 48, 90, 97, 142
Russell, B. A. W., 118–19, 120–1, 142
Ryle, Gilbert, 47, 48–50, 63, 84, 101, 117, 120, 142

Scepticism: about minds, 102–4; about objects, 116
Sellars, Wilfrid, 47, 48, 142
Sense data, 112–14, 117–18, 120–1
Setting oneself to, 47, 60, 63
Sherrington, 13n.
Shorter, J. M., 75n.
Shwayder, David, 12n., 142
Silber, R., 40, 142
Skills, 82–4
Smith, Carlota, 2n., 142
Stoutland, Frederick, 67, 142
Strawson, P. F., 12n., 114, 142

Taylor, Barry, 135–6n., 142
Taylor, Richard, 15n., 21, 47, 97, 142
Teleological basicness, 78–9, 81–8, 104
Thalberg, Irving, 2, 5, 24–5, 29–31, 41n., 75, 142
Thomson, J. Jarvis, 29, 142
Trying, 33–43, 46, 47, 58–9, 63–5, 72, 80n., 87, 88, 108–10, 112–13, 115–16, 122–3, 134; to move the body, 39–42, 45, 54–5

Vesey, G., 42, 143
Volitions, 47, 52, 54–5, 56–7, 62, 120

Wanting, 11, 41, 79–81
Warnock, Mary, 49, 143
Wiggins, David, vii, 134, 143
Wilkins, John, 13, 143
Williams, Bernard, vii, 37n., 41n., 59, 143
Willing, 14–15, 47, 54–5, 56–7, 60, 62, 63, 121
Wittgenstein, Ludwig, 23, 47, 59, 87, 112, 143
Wright, G. H. von, 21, 89, 90–4, 96, 143
Wright, Larry, 81, 143